THE PRINCIPLE & POWER OF

KINGDOM CITIZENSHIP

DESTINY IMAGE BOOKS BY DR. MYLES MUNROE

Applying the Kingdom

Applying the Kingdom 40-Day Devotional Journal

God's Big Idea

In Pursuit of Purpose

Kingdom Parenting

Kingdom Principles

Maximizing Your Potential

Maximizing Your Potential Expanded Edition

Myles Munroe 365-Day Devotional and Journal

Overcoming Crisis

Potential for Every Day

Purpose for Living

Reclaiming God's Original Purpose for Your Life

Rediscovering Faith

Rediscovering Kingdom Worship

Rediscovering the Kingdom Expanded Edition

Rediscovering the Kingdom 40-Day Devotional

Rediscovering the Kingdom CD set, volumes 1-5

Rediscovering the Kingdom DVD set, volumes 1-5

Releasing Your Potential

Releasing Your Potential Expanded Edition

Single, Married, Separated and Life after Divorce

Single, Married, Separated and Life after Divorce Expanded Edition

THE PRINCIPLE & POWER OF
KINGDOM CITIZENSHIP

keys to experiencing
HEAVEN *on* EARTH

the LEGACY *and* WISDOM *of*
Dr. Myles Munroe

DESTINY IMAGE® PUBLISHERS, INC.
P.O. Box 310, Shippensburg, PA 17257-0310
"Promoting Inspired Lives."

This book and all other Destiny Image and Destiny Image Fiction books are available at Christian bookstores and distributors worldwide.

Cover design by: Prodigy Pixel and Eileen Rockwell

For more information on foreign distributors, call 717-532-3040.
Reach us on the Internet: www.destinyimage.com.

ISBN 13 HC: 978-0-7684-0868-3
ISBN 13 TP: 978-0-7684-0930-7
ISBN 13 eBook: 978-0-7684-0869-0

For Worldwide Distribution, Printed in the U.S.A.
2 3 4 5 6 7 8 / 20 19 18 17 16

"The greatest tragedy in life is not death...
but life without a purpose."
—Dr. Myles Munroe

For a Christian statesman and Kingdom
revolutionary who pursued purpose with all of his
being, we are honored to present
The Principle and Power of Kingdom Citizenship,
by DR. MYLES MUNROE.

CONTENTS

INVITATION TO KINGDOM CITIZENSHIP

Most of us believe that we are from the planet Earth. And why not? Surely we're not from Mars or Venus or some other planet.

We and billions of other people live in hundreds of different countries, large and small, that cover the face of the Earth. We order our lives according to the governments and cultures of those countries. We eat the food that the earth provides and we raise our families. It's all we've ever known and it's all our parents and grandparents and great-grandparents ever knew. We believe that we are stuck with what Earth has to offer. We limit our whole lives to what's on the planet because that's the way everybody has been living for thousands of years.

However—we have lost touch with reality.

Even those of us who claim to know the ultimate King (God) do not understand that we also belong to a country that supersedes any of the human countries we know about. We think of "the Kingdom of God" as a term that's been pasted into prayers and sermons like an add-on. We don't consider it our home country any more than Mars. We think the Kingdom of God and Heaven comprise some kind of invisible future destination above the clouds.

The truth about the Kingdom is difficult to get across to people. I always feel as if I'm battling against 1,800 years of mental block. We've been so conditioned to think "religion," that God has difficulty getting through to us the real message He has delivered to us through Jesus Christ, which is about His Kingdom and how much He wants us to be full citizens of it, even while we're still living on this globe.

His message is personal. Anybody who claims Christ as Savior becomes a citizen of the Kingdom of God, but too many people leave their citizenship on the shelf. They consider their faith to be religion, not citizenship, and they don't realize that it should be making a difference in every detail of their personal, earthly lives.

You cannot see citizenship; you must experience it. In the same way, you cannot see the Kingdom of God; you must experience it.

This book is a training guide for citizens of the Kingdom. It will help you learn about your new country. I want you not only to understand everything you can about your new country, I also want you to accept the idea that you're living in it now, just as you have accepted the idea that Heaven is a real place where you can go after you die. The Kingdom of God and the Kingdom of Heaven are the same thing, you know.

God, the King, has set up His Kingdom so that it is composed of earthly outposts, or colonies, populated with His citizens. But the story of these colonies has not been an easy one. When Adam and Eve declared independence from Heaven, they had to set up their own government. God's Holy Spirit was no longer their "governor," because they didn't want Him to be. So Heaven started to seem like someplace far away. We lost the language, the culture, the values, the morals, the convictions, and the lifestyle that should have been the standard for any earthly colony of the Kingdom. We became aliens to God.

Because He wanted to turn that around, He sent His Son Jesus to make sure we would know about the Kingdom again. Once we find out how we fit into the Kingdom of God, the whole thing gets reversed. We begin to feel like aliens on planet Earth. We begin to feel that we belong someplace else. We also begin to rediscover the present-day benefits that come with our heavenly citizenship.

You cannot see the Kingdom of God; you must experience it.

It is my great passion to introduce people to the fullness of their citizenship in this heavenly Kingdom. You will see as you read this book that the Kingdom of God has almost nothing to do with religion. Instead, it has everything to do with the King Himself—with replicating His character and reproducing His will on Earth. Maturing in their citizenship, Kingdom citizens grow to reflect their King's culture, values, morals, nature, and lifestyle.

"Kingdom" is not my idea—it's God's idea. I don't know why we ignore the obvious. Almost every book of the Bible has some reference to the Kingdom. Jesus talked about His Father's Kingdom all the time. But we do not. Instead, we talk about the Church and Christianity. I have a serious problem with people who define the Kingdom of God too narrowly, in terms of one denomination or a single ethnic expression of faith in Christ. Yet I have an equally serious problem with people who define it in mushy terms, as if almost everyone living on earth is a Kingdom citizen without even thinking about it.

Like the people who are profiled in the 11th chapter of the letter to the Hebrews, we should be looking instinctively for a better country. It is called Heaven. Every one of us misses Heaven, but most of us can't figure out what we're missing. I'm telling you, we are missing our home country. We miss the lifestyle of peace, love, and joy. We miss the place where the streets are paved with gold and nobody has to steal it. We miss the place where the crystal-clear air is filled with joyful singing instead of smoke and gang violence. We miss our heavenly Father and our older Brother, not to mention all of our other brothers and sisters who belong to the King. We miss all of that, and somehow we think we must wait many years before we can go there.

The Kingdom of God is a present-tense place. It is an exciting place to call home. We have a lot to learn about it. Let's begin to explore together!

CHAPTER 1

UNDERSTANDING THE CONCEPT OF KINGDOMS

The pursuit of power is one of the most significant motivations of the human heart. The passionate desire to manage one's circumstances and environment seems to be built into the entire human race.

To the best of their ability, people work hard to control and improve their surroundings. Within any culture, people learn the "rules of the road" so that they can either follow them—or break them. Even acts of rebellion or aggression, whether isolated to a single individual or initiated by an organized army of soldiers, can trace their origin to this desire to control and dominate.

Young children cry and squabble to get the things they need and want. When a boy climbs his first tree, he is seeking to conquer new territory. When a girl picks a bouquet of flowers, she is trying to create something beautiful. As children mature, they gain knowledge about the world around them, and they put that know-how to use, striving not only to survive but to thrive.

This innate urge to manage the prevailing circumstances causes people to band together to accomplish things. Starting with family units, people organize themselves into towns, cities, geographical regions, and nations. They identify themselves as residents and citizens of the places where they live and work. Together, they share resources, face challenges, and train their children to do the same.

In a true kingdom, every single thing becomes part of the king's personal property

Where did this pursuit of power come from? Why does this trait manifest itself so consistently over the centuries, regardless of the color of a person's skin, gender, age and maturity, education level, skills, economic situation, or family of origin?

I am convinced that it is because the whole human race, individually and collectively, was created to exercise management over its prevailing circumstances. And in order to understand ourselves better and to identify how we fit into the big picture, we must first understand the concept of kingdoms and how kingdoms work.

ALL KINGS HAVE TERRITORY— AND EXTEND IT

Anything called a *kingdom* is a place where someone called a *king* has *dominion* over something. No king can have dominion unless he can claim ownership over territory. For centuries, kings vied for territory all over Europe. They could call themselves kings or lords because they owned vast acreages of land, and whatever was in the land became their property (their kingdom). Every field of barley, road, and river, every fox and tree and rat belonged to them.

Whenever one king grew strong enough to invade another king's property, he could extend his holdings. The greatness of his kingdom was measured by the amount of land he possessed. Kings formed armies of soldiers to protect their territory and to invade neighboring regions. The armies were funded by the resources of the king, and in the same way the farmers who worked the land depended on the king's largesse, even as they turned over most of their crops and livestock to him.

Nothing in the experience of modern governments equips us to understand this. The president of the United States does not own the whole country. The prime minister of England does not own the country he governs, and neither does the Queen. But in a true kingdom, every single thing becomes part of the king's personal property, every mountain, all of the roads, the animals and plants, the food and the water. No king can claim rulership unless he possesses some territory, which makes all kings products of their property.

The glory of a kingdom is determined by the size of the king's territory. That is why kings love to expand their kingdoms. The history of kingdoms is a story of expansion. A king must have territory. He must have something to rule. He must be wealthy and strong and decisive. And he must desire to be the king. No part-time or reluctant kings need apply for the job.

The king embodies the essence of his kingdom. The kingdom issues forth from him. His relative permanence instills confidence. May I suggest that your president or prime minister does not embody your country? He is not permanent enough. In fact, he has a part-time job. That's right. A democracy or a republic is not the same as a kingdom. If you are looking for stability and consistency, you do not want to put your faith in somebody who will be in charge for only four years or so. Your mortgage has twenty-five or thirty years on it. Wouldn't you like someone to be in charge at least longer than your mortgage?

The king is the center of a kingdom. He is the heart of it. People have to obey a king. He is the sovereign, and you do not argue with him or vote him out of office. We know what it is like to disagree with our elected officials. In fact, we tend to disagree quite loudly, and we broadcast it on the news. But disagreement with a king puts you in peril for your life. You do not have to like what he says, but you have to obey if you expect to stick around.

A kingdom can be good, bad or, most of the time, a little of both. Why did the kingdom model turn out to be such a typical form of government?

REDISCOVERING THE FIRST COUNTRY

The things we can see and experience turn out to be the evidence of unseen governing influences, yet little do we know what we are dealing with. We see both beauty and ugliness, joy and suffering, harmony and conflict. "That's just life," we say. In reality, we have two worlds on one planet. The Earth is the name of the planet, and the two worlds that contend with each other are actual kingdoms—the kingdom of darkness and the kingdom of light.

The kingdom of darkness has a ruler, and he stands in opposition to the ruler of the kingdom of light. Satan is one of the names people have given to the prince of darkness. The word "prince" means simply ruler, first or fundamental ruler. On the other side, people call the Son of God "the light of the world" or the ruler of the heavenly government.

Did you know that in Hebrew the word for "darkness" is the same as the word for "ignorance"? Similarly, the word for "knowledge" in Hebrew and Greek is the same as the word for "light." So when we talk about the world or kingdom of darkness and the world of light or Kingdom of God, we are not talking about light bulbs on or light bulbs off. We are talking about ignorance and knowledge. The prince of darkness is the prince of ignorance. He rules by your ignorance. Wherever you are ignorant, he can gain a foothold. Because of these two unseen kingdoms, we are living in a world that is always tense with ongoing territorial conflicts of interest.

We are living in a world that is always tense with ongoing territorial conflicts of interest.

The way I see it is this: the ruler of the kingdom of light created the physical place called the Earth in order to extend the Kingdom of Heaven. He created it so that the people He was about to create would have something to rule over on His behalf. I believe that the Earth was formed so that human beings could exercise co-rulership, so that they could become regents for the King in Heaven. I also believe that Heaven is a real place, and that it is the first real country, the original one, and that all other kingdoms since the beginning of time have been mere shadows of the Kingdom (which I distinguish with an uppercase K because it belongs to God).

In many ways, we can say that God was setting up a colony on earth, much as strong and wealthy countries have colonized parts of the earth. I know a lot about being part of a colony, because I am a native of the Bahamas, which was a colony of Great Britain until 1973. I was born under colonial rule. (We will talk more about colonization in the next chapter.)

But this heavenly colonization effort is still a work in progress. Most of what we see around us is the evidence of numerous conflicts between the colony of the kingdom of light and the kingdom of darkness. We will be learning how this works in the chapters of this book.

SUBSTITUTE KINGDOMS

When you serve under a king in a kingdom, you have the power to dominate your territory and to manage your assignment. What happens, however, if you lose your position? By nature, you are still a manager. Now you have been deprived of what you were managing. You have no purpose anymore. When that happens—and it happens all the time—people latch onto whatever makes them feel comfortable and at least partially in charge of the challenges around them.

One of the biggest fallbacks is—you guessed it—religion. If you cannot change your situation and you are trying hard to reconcile yourself to it, religion does a great job of helping. It makes you happy in your poverty, content in your illness, satisfied in your depression, and almost peaceful in your frustration. It works because it tells you that everything will be all right by and by. Your life will improve later. Religion tells you that Heaven is your destination, and all you have to do is hold out until you die. Religion postpones your reality to the future. It makes itself very attractive because it helps you accept things as they are when you feel you have lost control over your circumstances.

I am mentioning religion because I do not want you to get off on the wrong track about the Kingdom. Religion is not the same as the Kingdom I am talking about. It is a substitute. I know that both "Kingdom of God" and "Kingdom of Heaven" sound religious, but the Kingdom is something higher than any religion in the world.

If the Kingdom of God is not the same as religion, what is it? Let's put together what we know already and see what we come up with. We have determined that a kingdom involves a king having dominion over actual territory, and that the original territory, or the first country, of the Kingdom of God is Heaven. So a kingdom is a government and the Kingdom of God is God's government.

To that I added the fact that a king's decisions affect his territory and its citizens. A king is sovereign. He does not need to consult anyone else or get their votes. In other words, his will can become law. If he is a wicked, self-serving king, his expressed will can mean that the citizens will suffer. Just think what happened when people did not obey the expressed will of ancient kings. One moment he could be lavishing a fortune on them and the next moment he could say, "off with their heads!"

For better or for worse then, a king's decisions and decrees produce the quality of life of his subjects. Over time, the king's declarations produce a culture for the citizens of the kingdom.

It may be a culture of fear and poverty or it may be a culture of freedom and peace.

WHAT IS A KINGDOM?

By basic definition, then, any kingdom can be defined as follows:

> A kingdom is the governing influence of a king over a territory, impacting that territory with his will, his purpose, and his intent, producing a culture and a moral standard for his citizens.

A kingdom is definitely a governmental system, but a kingdom is not a democracy or a republic. The king's word is law, and he does not need to share his power with other branches of government. He *is* the government. He is the sole and final authority. He is the law, the court, the judge, the cabinet, the congress, and the parliament. He is the head of state, the president, and the prime minister. And he does not have to worry about term limits. Nobody votes for or against him, because in a kingdom, nobody votes. Referendums are unheard of in a kingdom.

From our national culture as well as from our religious culture, we sometimes get the notion that we can exercise our vote for or against one of the King's laws or decisions. But it doesn't work that way!

The king has influence over his territory and he rules over it. This means that he rules over the people who dwell there, the ones who are the citizens of his territory. He looks after them. He organizes them to function as a society.

Now most of you who will be reading this book have been raised in countries that are considered democracies or republics. Even in countries with a king or queen, like England, the governing power and authority does not reside solely in that one person. It can be very difficult for most of us to wrap our minds around the concept of living as a citizen of a kingdom.

Our idea of the kingdom concept is insufficient, to say the least. From our national culture as well as from our religious culture, we sometimes get the notion that we can exercise our vote for or against one of the King's laws or decisions. But it doesn't work that way! Even when highly respected religious leaders vote, for example, to promote a practicing homosexual into a position of high authority, they cannot change the moral standard of the King or His true Kingdom. The King of the original country (Heaven) is God, and He is the highest King of them all.

CHARACTERISTICS OF A KINGDOM

All kingdoms share specific characteristics. As you read through this list, you will find yourself nodding in agreement, "Yes, I knew that...." It seems so obvious when you see the facts. How could we have missed it for so long? We will be discussing most of these in detail in the chapters of this book. Here are the characteristics of a kingdom, any kingdom, whether an earthly one or the heavenly one:

- All kingdoms have a king. Kings are born into kingship, not nominated and elected.

- All kingdoms have a lord, which means an owner. The lord and king are the same.

- The king's power is absolute in a true kingdom.

- All kingdoms have territory. The king must have a domain.

- The king personally owns everything in his domain.

- The king is never voted out of power in a kingdom.

- All kingdoms are a country, a nation, and they are different from each other.

- All kingdoms have a constitution, a covenant that the king makes with his own citizens.

- All kingdoms consist of a group of people who identify themselves with a sovereign.

- All kingdoms have laws. Laws are the strict principles by which the citizens must live.

- All kingdoms have citizens. Citizenship entails certain responsibilities and it bestows specific rights and privileges.

- All kingdoms have royal privileges to which the citizens can have access through royal favor.

- All kingdoms have a principle of royal favor.

- All kingdoms have a code of ethics.

- All kingdoms have common wealth, which is why they are often called a "commonwealth"; the citizens have access to the same supply of wealth.

- Along the same lines, all kingdoms discourage private ownership.

- All kingdoms have a culture. This has to do with their lifestyle, clothing, values and morals, food, and even the way people respond to problems.

- All kingdoms have an economy.

- All kingdoms have a taxation system.

- All kingdoms have a principle of giving to the king. Citizens never come before their king empty-handed.

- All kingdoms have an army. (The soldiers are not civilians or ordinary citizens. In the Kingdom of God, you cannot see the army because it consists of angels.)

- The king's presence is the same as the king's authority. The king's name is the essence of his authority.

- All kingdoms have delegated authority.

- A king embodies the government of his kingdom. The government is not divided into branches or departments.

- All kingdoms have an educational system.

- All kingdoms have administration and organization.

- All kingdoms have a principle of glory, related to the sovereign king. The citizenry represents its king's glory.

- Similarly, all kingdoms have a principle of worship, directed toward the king but beneficial to the worshippers.

- All kingdoms have principles of reputation and provision. (This means that, for the sake of his reputation, the king must meet the needs of his citizens.)

- All kingdoms have a principle of decree. (Kings do not need to debate proposed laws, and their decrees cannot be changed.)

- Kings can choose their own citizens.

Without knowing the big picture, most of us get involved in all of our rituals and we forget about our relationship with our Creator. We think that everything begins and ends with us.

People are looking for qualities such as these. They would like a new economy. They would like to live under different laws. They want to experience royal favor and privileges. This is the kind of kingdom we are all seeking. Even though all of us will remain subject to the restrictions of whatever country and municipality we belong to as long as we are alive on the planet Earth, we retain an instinctive passion for something bigger and better, some kind of kingdom of light and goodness.

THE BIG PICTURE

If you do not understand the big picture of what God intended for the earth and its citizens, you cannot understand your small part of the whole story. What did God really want to accomplish when He created countless solar systems, millions of planets, and billions of stars? What was He thinking about when He made one of those solar systems with nine planets (or eight, if we can't count Pluto anymore)? What was His intent when he chose the third planet from that solar system's sun and put life on that planet? And what was He thinking about when He decided to put a piece of Himself into a "dirt suit" on that planet, creating something called man? What was He thinking about; what was He after?

Meantime, here on earth, what is the point of staying alive? Are we born just to make a living, reproduce by having a child or two, and eventually die? Without knowing the big picture, most of us get involved in all of our rituals and we forget about our relationship with our Creator. We think that everything begins and ends with us. We are always scrambling to stay on top. Our lives never seem to have very much meaning.

If, however, you understand that the created universe stems from a parallel universe called Heaven, and that the Creator is a King who is always extending His territory, you can begin to recognize that you are part of a family business. In fact, being part of that family business gives you significance.

> *The Kingdom is a family business and our Father wants to extend His business into foreign territories. He wants His kids like you and me to run the Earth Department for Him.*

All human beings are searching for some kind of significance, and their search manifests itself in many ways. All religions attempt to answer the Big Picture questions. All the conflicts between religions come from the competing searches. It is not just the Buddhists, the Hindus, the Muslims, the Christians, and the other major or minor religions; even the agnostics and the atheists are part of the same search.

The search is not bad, but as we know very well, the search often becomes its own answer. We stop searching and make the means the end. We get defensive about our own version of the search and protective of our particular rituals. We set ourselves apart as members of our own particular group. We miss the fact that there is more.

We are the King's kids. The King has been inviting us to realize that we are His children and to become full citizens of the biggest, richest, most glorious Kingdom we can imagine, and we have not heard His invitation. Instead, we have been fooling around like street urchins in some vacant lot, trying to change it into a playground.

The Kingdom is a family business and our Father wants to extend His business into foreign territories. He wants His kids like you and me to run the Earth Department for Him. His intention was to have the Earth Department look a lot like the Headquarters. He wants to extend His experience from the invisible world to the visible world through his family members. He wants His Kingdom to come and His will to be done on earth as it is in Heaven.

The book will tell you what you want to know if you want to become part of the most important family business of all time.

CHAPTER 2

THE COLONY

I am a citizen of the Commonwealth of the Bahamas. The Bahamas is an island nation in the Caribbean Sea that used to be a colony of Great Britain. All of the Caribbean island nations have colonization as part of their history—the Bahamas, Jamaica, Barbados, Saint Kitts and Nevis, Saint Thomas, Saint Lucia, Saint Vincent, Grenada, all the way down to Trinidad and Tobago, almost too many islands to count. Many of these islands are former colonies of Great Britain, and some of them are still British territories today.

The fact that I was born and grew up under colonial rule means that I am intimately acquainted with what it means to be a successful colony of another nation.

What is a colony? A colony is a territory that is under the direct control of a central, imperialistic government. The government, which was England in our case, considers the colony an outpost of the faraway central authority. Great Britain is on the other side of the Atlantic Ocean, 7000 kilometers (4300 miles) away, but those of us who lived in their territory of the Bahamas were considered English citizens.

Why do we speak English in the Bahamas and not some other language? Because of the British. Why do we use "the king's English" and not American English, even though the United States is much closer to our shores? Because of our status as a British colony for two hundred years. Generations of Bahamians were educated in that particular type of English, and all of our business is transacted in that language. Despite the fact that over 90 percent of our population is of African descent, our ancestors having been brought to the islands as slaves to work on the plantations, very few of us know even a few words in our ancestors' native language, or their customs. You can tell that my ancestors came from Africa, but I know next to nothing about African history. Instead, I learned in school about Sir Francis Drake and Sir Walter Raleigh and Oliver Cromwell. I learned the names of all of the long succession of English kings and queens. I read all of the plays of Shakespeare.

Great Britain gave Bahamians other distinctive features, as well. They gave us their long socks and short pants; they gave us neckties; they gave us a preference for straightened hair; they gave us knives and forks; they gave us their tea. When you drive a car in the Bahamas, you must drive on the left side of the road as you would in England, and for the most part you will be driving on narrow roads that cross each other with British-style roundabouts. The colonial influence is very obvious in the Bahamas.

You can find colonial influences wherever you go in the world. The first time I went to Suriname, which is not too far from the Bahamas on the north side of South America, I thought I had landed in Holland. I wanted to speak with a black man in the airport, but we could not communicate because he understood Dutch only. He was fluent only in the language of his nation's former monarch, and so was I, and the two languages were not the same.

A kingdom is not just a piece of real estate. It has a culture. It has morals and standards. It has values. And they get exported to the colonies of that particular kingdom.

ESTABLISHED STANDARDS

A kingdom is a nation under a king's rule, which means that the king himself establishes the standards for the country and its colonies. My wife and I saw a good illustration of this when we went to France. While we were there, we toured the Palace of Versailles, the vast château of King Louis XIV. We were told about how the king decreed that the length of his royal foot was henceforth known as the standard 12-inch foot. Other people's feet were smaller or larger than his, but his foot became the rule.

Today the French use the metric system, but when King Louis XIV was on the throne, they did not. The king established the standards, and everybody was compelled to follow them. To this day, schoolchildren use a straight measuring stick of a specific length, and it is called a "ruler." They use it to measure things and to draw straight lines. They do not get to discuss or change the standard. They just have to accommodate themselves to it.

To reiterate the definition I used in the first chapter, a kingdom is the governing influence of a king over a territory, impacting that territory with his will, his purpose, and his intent, producing a culture and a moral standard for his citizens. In other words, a kingdom is not just a piece of real estate. It has a culture. It has morals and standards. It has values. And they get exported to the colonies of that particular kingdom. By definition, a colony is a group of citizens established in a foreign territory to influence that dominion for their home government.

In terms of the Kingdom of God, you could say that when you come into the Kingdom, you change colonies. But it can take a long time to lose your old ways of thinking and behaving just as in the Bahamas, where our culture to this day is saturated with British ways despite years of independence as a sovereign nation. When you come into the Kingdom, your personal life will carry many of your old ways as you learn to think and behave differently to match your new affiliation.

Regardless of where we live on the globe, those of us who are citizens of the Kingdom of Heaven were born as colonists of the kingdom of darkness. But somewhere along the line we switched loyalties, joining forces with colonists of the kingdom of light. When we switched, we began to shed our old habits and worldview, along with our old ways of thinking and our expectations. In time, we should begin not only to represent our new King, but to resemble Him.

When people become colonists in the Kingdom of God, they sign up for a steep learning curve, but it's worth it. You may or may not know what I am talking about from personal experience. The fact of the matter is that unless we learn what it means to be a citizen of this earth-colony of the Kingdom of Heaven, we will miss out on all of the benefits that come with colonial status.

"OCCUPY"

What I am trying to explain is how colonization describes both a king's expansion of his kingdom territory as well as an expression of his personality. Colonization means that a kingdom has been extended to a distant territory, and after a time the colony can be expected to manifest the culture of the kingdom, even though the citizens possessed a different culture in their past.

When people become colonists in the Kingdom of God, they sign up for a steep learning curve, but it's worth it.

Colonization does not always work out. Here is a 2000-year-old parable about some of the difficulties of Kingdom colonization. It begins like this:

> *A certain nobleman went into a far country to receive for himself a kingdom, and to return. And he called his ten servants, and delivered them ten pounds, and said unto them, Occupy till I come. (Luke 19:12-13, KJV)*

The "far country" is a new colony. The man went to that territory because he was supposed to receive kingship there.

He left ten of his servants behind, giving them resources and telling them to transact business until he returned. "Occupy" is a word that implies not only staying behind to represent the owner, but actively conducting business. The nobleman wanted his servants to administrate and take control of the business in the place, and he told them that he would come back to check on them.

As you read the rest of the parable an unhappy story unfolds that looks like the story of humankind on earth. The nobleman-king gets rejected by the citizens of the new country—and at the same time the ones to whom he entrusted his business dealings let him down badly. True, some of the servants succeed in their business dealings to varying degrees, but at least one of them refused to do anything at all with the money his master left with him; he hid it away inside a piece of cloth and left it there the whole time his master was gone. Did the king appreciate this? Not at all. He swiftly exercised his sovereign power to punish both the unworthy servant and the rebellious colonists.

It did not have to turn out that way, but the citizens and the servants chose to repudiate their master's wishes. When he came to claim his kingship, they excommunicated him from the colony territory; they told him they did not want him. Isn't this just what we have done in many of our countries today? We have taken God out of our schools and universities, out of our government. In the Bahamas we haven't decided to erect a legal separation of God and government and I hope we don't ever do it, but in many other countries, that is the law.

The servants in the parable were instructed to "occupy" because their territory was never created to be governed without the king. But they did not. They took matters into their own hands, and the result was ruin. The stewards in the story blame their actions on their circumstances, and even on the master himself. "For I feared you, because you are an austere man. You collect what you did not deposit, and reap what you did not sow" (Luke 19:21). This sounds a lot like what the King God finds when He checks on the people He left to occupy the planet for Him. We say this to God: "We think you are too harsh. We can't trust you, and we prefer to do things our own way."

The King is still bringing in the Kingdom, one colonist at a time.

How has the earth colony turned out? Just look around you. Does earth look like Heaven? Look at the bars on our windows and the guns in our houses. Every day a murder. We are afraid to jog outside, so we buy a treadmill. We are afraid to let our children visit certain family members, lest they be abused. We are unable to succeed in marriage, so the divorce business is booming. We have got nothing to show the King except broken lives, disease, depression, conflict, religious clashes, war, frustration, bankruptcy, tyrants and dictators, broken homes, and broken nations.

Is it too late for us? I don't think so. The King is still bringing in the Kingdom, one colonist at a time. Yet the only way we can occupy until He comes again is to change. We must recognize that we cannot do it on our own. We need the King to save us from ourselves. We need a Savior to save us, to salvage the colony. He is coming to bring in a new government—if we will accept it. We should realize by now that none of the governments human beings have produced are working: democracy, democratic socialism, communism... none of them. That is because they all belong to the kingdom of darkness, with which people have affiliated since our earliest ancestors first declared independence from the original King.

Referring back to the parable, we need to realize that the King will be asking us to give Him an account. He will not care how your pastor did or how your boss did. He will want to know what *you* did with the resources He gave you to oversee. He has questions for you. "I want to know how you have been doing," He says. "What have you done to represent my Kingdom? How have you explained and expanded my Kingdom to the people in your environment? Have you demonstrated integrity in your workplace? Have you been a good father or mother or child or friend? Have you made things better in your circle of influence? What was your attitude? Are you making investments with what I have given you? What kind of job are you doing?"

The fact is, those of us who are known as Kingdom colonists are not earthlings; we are "heavenlings" or "heavenians," if there can be such words. We are citizens of the Kingdom of Heaven. Many of us learned a prayer that includes these words: "Your kingdom come. Your will be done on earth as it is in heaven" (Matt. 6:10). When we pray it, we are expecting the Father's will to be performed in our colony, just as it is in Heaven. We are acting out of our identity as true colonists who see themselves as full citizens of Heaven and representatives of the King.

CITIZENSHIP VS. MEMBERSHIP

Most organized groups within societies, including religions, function on the basis of membership. However, countries, nations, kingdoms—and their colonies—are different, because they function on the basis of citizenship. This is an important distinction to make, because otherwise you might assume that being part of a colony relegates you to some kind of second-class citizenship that is more like membership in a club.

You need to know that you are a full citizen of whatever nation claims your territory as a colony. This applies even to Heaven and Earth. Heaven is the territory of the King called God, although it remains largely invisible to human eyes. Heaven is God's country, if you want to call it that. Heaven is an actual place. Sometimes people who have visited it give us a glimpse of what it is like, and they report amazing experiences. Heaven is God's headquarters. His throne is there. (The word "throne" does not mean just a fancy chair. It means a "seat of power" or citadel.)

You will hear two terms used interchangeably: the Kingdom of God and the Kingdom of Heaven. They both mean the same thing except that the first one is referring to the One who owns the Kingdom and the other is referring to the territory.

That is where we get some of our descriptive terms for God. People call Him the King of glory, the King of Creation, the King of the Universe. He is the King of everything seen as well as everything unseen. He owns it all and He rules it from within His original territory, Heaven.

Often, those of us who dwell on the planet called Earth fail to understand the setup. We see the physical planet all around us, and we find it to be delightful and fearful at the same time. We may recognize the existence of a world outside of our immediate experience, but we do not understand its importance. We recognize our citizenship in some nation, but we do not realize that all of us possess dual citizenship—in a physical country or colony and in an unseen one.

The fact is, those of us who are known as Kingdom colonists are not earthlings; we are "heavenlings."

Since Kingdom of God is a country, a real place called Heaven, and since countries bestow citizenship on the people who dwell there, it is citizenship (not membership) that has been bestowed on the "heavenlings" who dwell on the colony called Earth. Citizenship comes with more guarantees and privileges than membership does, along with specific responsibilities.

You can become a member of a *community* within your colony or country, but your citizenship is what ties you to the community in the first place. In the same way, you can become a member of a religion or a branch of a religion, but your citizenship in the kingdom of light (or, sad to say, the kingdom of darkness) will take priority over your membership in that particular religion.

Naturalized citizenship is the goal, not mere membership, whether you live in the primary country or one of its colonies. You need to pursue full citizenship in the Kingdom of Heaven as if your life depended upon it, because it does. As a citizen, you will grow to reflect the culture of the country, which in turn reflects the ruler of the country. Your life will be radically changed and improved as a result.

Citizenship is a legal position. Membership is more of an accommodation. You can apply for membership in the local lodge or Rotary Club and they can decide whether or not to accommodate and include you. They can also decide to de-member (I could have written dis-member) you, making you a non-member. But once you are a citizen, no one can take away your citizenship just because they don't like you, not even the government. (You can read how this applies to a citizen of the Kingdom of Heaven in John 10:28-29.)

Having legal citizenship entitles you to certain rights, and those rights do not depend on feelings or emotions; they depend on much more powerful things: position and law. You can switch religious affiliations or other memberships without losing your citizenship in the Kingdom, and people do. They get their feelings hurt or they offend somebody, so they move on. They change their minds about what they want to do, so they find a new place that will accommodate their viewpoint.

THE DECLARATION OF INDEPENDENCE

Now even though a country will not remove your name from the citizenship rolls, a citizen can remove his own name if he or she chooses. In any kind of kingdom, that is called rebellion, and it happens all the time. When the American colonists wrote their Declaration of Independence, they were announcing their intention to renounce their English citizenship, to break off legal ties with that country, to establish their own independent nation.

Once you are a citizen, no one can take away your citizenship just because they don't like you, not even the government.

Independence and private ownership are an abomination within a colony. They cannot coexist with a kingdom mentality. To this day, the "American spirit" is the same as a spirit of independence, and a strong streak of individualism and private ownership has resulted in the growth of capitalism and its inherent conflicts.

When the first man declared independence from his government in the Garden, he resigned his citizenship by switching it to the kingdom of darkness. (Remember what I wrote in chapter 1—darkness is synonymous with ignorance. Adam was ignorant of the importance of obedience to the single legal regulation of his government, and he was ignorant of the goals of his government.)

A declaration of independence results in the loss of citizenship. You may not even know what you are doing, but the end result is the same. If you change your mind, you may decide to seek citizenship again, and you may eventually be repatriated. But it will not be easy to regain your citizenship once you have lost it.

Just a note here about what the human race lost when the first human being declared his independence from his original King. We need to know what we are looking for if we ever hope to regain it. The human race did not lose residence in Heaven. The first human was created on earth and out of the earth. His residence was on earth. He never resided in Heaven and he did not fall from Heaven. He was the original colonist, and he had been allotted full citizenship in the Kingdom of Heaven even as he dwelt on the earth. What he repudiated was his *assignment*, which was to exercise dominion over the earth in obedience to the King. When he refused to follow God's directions in fulfilling his assignment, that first man lost dominion and citizenship at the same time.

As the story goes, Adam's wife, Eve, was persuaded by a talking serpent, otherwise known as the devil, to eat some delicious-looking fruit from one of the trees in their garden paradise. Trouble was, that was the one and only thing their Creator-King, God, had instructed them *not* to do. They had only one rule and they broke it. So they got kicked out of their garden, and all of their children, grandchildren, and so forth were born outside of the colony territory—which means that none of them were born into citizenship in the Kingdom of Heaven.

Because of what the first man did, every one of the 7.3 billion people on earth and the 259,000 who were born last night are hungry for the Kingdom of God. It is not about going to Heaven someday (although most religions think so); it is about becoming repatriated into the Kingdom that our long-ago forefather lost. It is about resuming exercise of the dominion over the planet, expanding the original colony until it covers the entire globe.

In the Garden, the first man had it all. He had every provision and all the privileges that come with the assignment of stewardship and management. The Garden was the first settlement of the colony of Heaven, and the Fall changed all that. We call this "the Fall" and yet we do not really think very much about what those first humans fell from. Innocence? Goodness?

Obedience? Yes, but more importantly they fell from dominion. They fell down on the job by breaking the one rule or law they had been given. For two bites of fruit, they lost their citizenship in the colony of the Kingdom of Heaven. Through the Fall, Earth was disconnected from Heaven. No longer did Adam defer to the direction of God.

> *It is about resuming exercise of the dominion over the planet, expanding the original colony until it covers the entire globe.*

When you cut off the relationship with your kingdom, you have to set up your own government. Independence can be hard to live out. Ever since we declared our independence in the Bahamas, we no longer refer to England to make governmental decisions. We had to start running our own country. We encountered endless problems that we never come across before, and we had to figure out what to do on our own.

HIGH TREASON

The first man's decision to disregard God's prohibition and to eat of the fruit of the tree seems like such a minor thing. But God regarded it as high treason. Treason involves deceit and corruption. The highest form of trust has been broken. Adam not only disobeyed the one rule he had been given, he lied about it afterward.

If an ambassador of a country should sell the secrets of his country to another country, that is treason. In every country in the world, treason is punishable by death. That is why God, when He gave Adam the whole world to run, entrusted all of it to his stewardship, but gave him the one single prohibition, and leveled with him about the potential punishment: "You must not eat from the tree of the knowledge of good and evil, for when you eat from it you will certainly die" (Gen. 2:17, NIV).

The pronouncement of the punishment of death revealed the gravity of the sin. The word sin means rebellion against authority. Now Adam and all of the individuals who followed him would find death inevitable. He had committed treason. The man himself could not undo the punishment. A new Adam would have to come from Heaven to do that, and He did. He came to restore what Adam lost—everything.

THE GOVERNOR OF THE COLONY

When the Bahamas was still a colony, the Queen hardly ever came here. In all my life, I think she visited twice. And yet she was our ruler. This shows how a sovereign does not have to come into the territory in order to claim it or retain it. What she did was to send a man called a governor to live here. As long as he was here, the queen was represented here. A succession of governors lived in a big pink mansion known as the Government House on Duke Street in Nassau.

Naturally, when a colony declares independence from the home country, the appointed governor must leave. Here, this happened peacefully, but in other colonies it happens with violence. Then the newly independent government must set up its own structure and rules. As the new country adjusts to its sovereign status, many citizens may long for the "good old days" when they were under colonial rule. Others will be perfectly happy forging an independent existence and creating a distinctive culture.

A new Adam would have to come from Heaven to do that, and He did. He came to restore what Adam lost—everything.

How does governorship translate into the Kingdom of Heaven and its expanding colony on earth? First of all, the native population cannot assume the colonial governorship role, although they can be loyal citizens. That role is reserved for a special, divine representative of the heavenly country known as the Holy Spirit. The earth-colony was never intended to function without its heavenly governor, but when humankind declared independence, He had to leave. The citizens lost their legal connection to their first country, Heaven. They threw off its constitution and rulership and culture.

As a result, we have inherited a mess. Our world today is a culture of death. We have become citizens of a country (the whole earth) that, minus the stabilizing influence of Heaven, has gone completely berserk. Fighting within our homes and waging wars overseas, we keep trying to control the out-of-control situation we find ourselves in, but we can't agree about how to do it. Can we get our first governor back?

Do you know the answer to our dilemma? Let's explore it some more together

CHAPTER 3

WHAT IS CITIZENSHIP?

I have visited over seventy countries, and my passport really gets a workout. Sometimes, even though I have all the right documentation, I run into difficulties with the customs officials. I suppose they are just doing their jobs, but I think they sometimes overdo their jobs. The interrogations can seem endless. When that happens, I feel like telling my interrogator, "Look, I come from the Bahamas, and you are making me want to go back home. Do you realize what a wonderful place the Bahamas is? The average Bahamian citizen has everything. We have everything cool, man. No harassment." Times like that make me appreciate the benefits of my citizenship.

Back in the Bahamas, we have people from other Caribbean nations such as Haiti clamoring for citizenship. These people want to join themselves with our government or the government of nations like the United States; they are looking for some nearby jurisdiction that is better off than their own. Although Haiti is the oldest black republic in the world and the second-oldest republic in the Western hemisphere after the United States, it still struggles economically. Ordinary citizens face a multitude of problems. These are good people, but their governmental system seems to be defective. As is the case in other countries with problems, you will find a very small group of people who are rich and a vast majority who are very poor. For the average Haitian citizen, the benefits of citizenship are limited indeed. They are willing to uproot their families and start over. By some estimates, as many as 40,000 Haitians are now living in the Bahamas, and a very large proportion of that number may be illegal immigrants. They know that legal citizenship status can be hard to get and that people must want it badly enough to work for it. They know that Bahamian citizenship would provide them with opportunities they cannot have any other way.

By definition, a "citizen" is someone who owes allegiance to a government and who is therefore entitled to receive protection from mistreatment and also to enjoy special rights and privileges that come with citizenship. A citizen is automatically connected with the seat of power of his government. That is why people want to become citizens of successful and wealthy nations; once you are a citizen you can expect your life to improve. Why else would you want to go to all that trouble?

RIGHTS AND BENEFITS OF CITIZENSHIP

Citizenship is the most valuable asset of a nation. Because of its power, it is not easily given or obtained and the current citizens of a nation do not readily want to share citizenship with outsiders. We are seeing this play out in many Western European countries at the present time because of the continuing influx of immigrants from Muslim countries. Such a large population shift has the potential to transform the entire religious, social, and cultural complexion of Europe. Weekly, we hear of sectarian riots and legal power struggles. The Muslim immigrants would not be moving into those countries if they did not offer the prospect of a higher standard of living.

The benefits of citizenship in a country with a kingdom system of government can far outweigh the benefits of citizenship in even wealthy nations that have non-kingdom forms of government.

From the United States, we hear reports of Mexican immigration challenges. In spite of checkpoints and an actual fence on the U.S.-Mexican border, illegal immigrants pour into the southwestern states and move northward. Some legislators want to place all illegal aliens on a fast track to American citizenship. Others want to detain and deport them.

Citizenship is such a valuable status that people are willing to do wicked things to obtain it. They falsify documents or marry people they do not even know simply to get the advantages of citizenship. All immigrants, legal or otherwise, are seeking the privileges and benefits of the host country. They want jobs, higher pay, better health care, greater educational opportunities, and an overall better quality of life than they can obtain as citizens of their home countries. The best way to obtain improved benefits and rights is to become full citizens of a successful and well-to-do nation.

A citizen is part of an elite, privileged group, and people who were born into their citizenship do not appreciate their status as much as they could. Citizenship is easy to come by if you are born into it, but if you must seek naturalized citizenship you soon find out that it can be an arduous process. Citizenship status is too precious for governments to hand out indiscriminately like handbills.

You need to know that the benefits of citizenship in a country with a kingdom system of government can far outweigh the benefits of citizenship in even wealthy nations that have non-kingdom forms of government. This is because, ideally, the king's wealth will be distributed broadly to his citizens, whereas in a democratic country where capitalism prevails, not everyone can capitalize on the resources to the same degree. (In fact, poverty is necessary for capitalism to work, because you need "have-nots" to sell products and services to.)

THE COMMONWEALTH PRINCIPLE

The word "commonwealth" exists only in kingdoms. When the Bahamas was part of the Commonwealth of Great Britain, the British built our roads and provided us with clean water. They brought us electricity and other upgraded services. They had their warships anchored in Nassau harbor so they could protect us poor little Bahamians.

A citizen of a kingdom who is in good standing with a king has more than enough of everything.

When we decided to declare our independence, all of those types of assistance ceased. Independence means you have to manage your own affairs, pay your own bills, provide your own clean water, and maintain your own highway system. (Thus, our roads today are famous for being bumpy. We are no longer part of a commonwealth that pays for improvements.)

Because of the commonwealth principle, the citizenry in a kingdom begins to reflect their king's qualities, including his wealth. In extreme examples, you see something like the Palace of Versailles, which is so big that it would take three days to walk through all the rooms, with gold everywhere. It is the largest king's palace in the world. And that's just the house. King Louis XIV also had stables for his horses that were so extensive they would cover half of the Bahamas. Even today, those stables look better than the house I live in.

Three thousand people lived in the Palace of Versailles at any given time. They wanted to live there, of course, because everything was provided for them. The servant's quarters had marble floors. Free housing. Free food. Free clothes. Free everything. And when the king moved to his winter house—because the palace at Versailles was just his summer house—everything went with him, all three thousand people, six thousand horses, the gold—the whole government had to move.

A citizen of a kingdom who is in good standing with a king has more than enough of everything. The king sets the standards—and he makes it possible for his citizens to achieve them. Remember our definition of a kingdom: A kingdom is the governing influence of a king over a territory, impacting that territory with his will, his purpose, and his intent, producing a culture and a moral standard for his citizens. Notice...these benefits belong only to his citizens. Citizenship matters greatly. An individual's welfare depends on it.

THE POWER OF CITIZENSHIP

Citizenship empowers an individual; citizenship provides legitimate access to all the rights and privileges of a constitution and a country. Becoming a citizen, especially a citizen of a kingdom such as the Kingdom of God, means that you become powerful. Your citizenship is the source of your personal authority where those rights are concerned. You have the power to demand things. By the power of your citizenship, you can call in constitutional privileges and promises. The constitution is more powerful than the citizens, just as the law is more powerful than the lawyer or the judge that exercises it and certainly more powerful than the politicians who talk about it. Good citizens have access to the full protection and advantage of the law.

Remember what we learned in chapter 2 about citizenship vs. membership. Countries do not have members. You cannot be a member of the United States of America. You cannot be a member of Jamaica. You can certainly be a member of a religious group or an organization, but you would never say that you are a member of a country because membership does not entitle you to the full range of rights. Citizens have rights, and they do not have to pay membership dues to keep them. Citizenship is permanent, if you want it to be. Whether or not the people around you like you, you cannot be deprived of your constitutional rights by a consensus or somebody's whim. Once you are a citizen, you are no longer a mere member; you are a legal creature, which means the law protects you. You could even say that citizenship is dangerous. Law means you remove emotions and relationships out of the equation. It doesn't matter who you like or do not like, or who likes you. You are a citizen, regardless.

Citizens have rights, and they do not have to pay membership dues to keep them. Citizenship is permanent, if you want it to be. Citizenship is the most powerful gift that a government can give an individual.

You can learn the language of a country and still not have citizenship. You can obtain a working visa and earn money in a country and remain an alien. You can live for decades in a place and never become a citizen. Only by going all the way through the citizenship initiation process can you become a citizen. For your part as a citizen, you need to submit to the rules and regulations of your government. For the government's part, it agrees to take you in and give you powerful entitlements. You can only become a citizen when the government opts to make an agreement with you.

Behind citizenship lies a covenant—a legal contract or solemn agreement—between the government and each individual citizen. Citizens, in other words, have a contract with their government.

That citizenship covenant gives you so much power that you can even attack the government. Governments know this, which is one of the reasons they do not give citizenship to everybody who walks by the immigration office. Citizenship is the most powerful gift, to use the term broadly, that a government can give an individual. The constitution of the government guarantees certain valuable rights to its citizens, and each and every citizen has access to the same rights.

Citizens must maintain their access to those rights by complying with a common set of laws. When you move to another country, you do not bring your own laws with you. You must submit to that country's laws day in and day out if you expect to carry out your part of the bargain. All covenants or contracts have two parties, and the contract of citizenship is no exception. The citizen's part of the agreement is to comply with the law of the land.

Those rights are guaranteed to you. You do not have to beg for them. You do not have to bribe anybody to manipulate favor. Once you become a citizen of a country, you are responsible to the government to follow the laws. The government is responsible for protecting your rights, but you always remain accountable for your behavior. If you transgress, you may find yourself deprived of some of your rights for a while. When people go to prison, their citizenship does not get revoked, but some of the rights and privileges do—because they did not hold up their side of the contract as law-abiding citizens.

A government could give you a piece of property, and it would not be as secure as citizenship because they could take it back and expel you.

In a very real way, citizenship is power-sharing. A citizen shares the power of the government. Essentially, a citizen becomes one with the government. (A negative example of this power would be when an elected government suddenly extends citizenship to a group of people who will then vote them back into power.)

No greater honor can be bestowed on an individual than the honor or making him or her a citizen. A government could give you a piece of property, and it would not be as secure as citizenship because they could take it back and expel you. They could give you a visa to live in the country for six months, but at the end of that time, you would have to leave. They could give you a five-year working permit and yet you would not be able to exercise the rights of citizenship—and at any time during that five years, they could change their minds, write a new law, and tell you to go home immediately.

Citizenship is a privilege, after all. You can't just have it for the asking. Citizenship is not a right, but it is a privilege that gives you rights. You cannot demand it and you cannot hurry it up. I have spoken with people who have lived in the Bahamas for years and who have applied for citizenship, but they are still waiting. National policy varies from place to place, but the only quick way to become a citizen is to be born into it, either to be born within the borders of the particular country, or to be born elsewhere to parents who are legal citizens. Some people think it is just a piece of paper that has been stamped by the immigration office. It is a lot more than that. It is a piece of the country.

Citizenship is the conferring of a nation on an individual. They take the whole country and they put it on top of you. You walk in with nothing and you leave with everything on you.

Here is my best definition of citizenship:

Citizenship is the constitutional rights and privileges bestowed upon an individual, guaranteeing legal status to the individual, which is protected by the laws of the country.

CITIZEN AND PASSPORT-HOLDER

Once you are a citizen, you can obtain a passport that says so, and people will have to respect your citizenship everywhere you go because you have the whole power of your government behind you. As a matter of fact, your passport belongs to the government, not to you personally. It's a crime to deface it and you have to surrender it if the government tells you to do so. When an official asks to see your passport, that is the single confirmation of your citizenship that he wants to see. He does not want your birth certificate or your driver's license. Your passport tells him that you are a citizen. In most cases, he will ask you a few questions about what you intend to do in his country, and then he will stamp it and wave you through. That passport means that he has to treat you right.

On my passport, I can read something like this: "Allow the bearer of this document to pass freely without let or hindrance and afford the bearer such assistance and protection as may be necessary." When I return to the country of my citizenship, my passport will let me get back in without any problem, either.

My citizenship goes with me wherever I go. I do not have to go to my country or stay in my country to be a citizen.

You may not be able to drive a car or vote in an election until you reach a certain age, but you will be considered a citizen from day one of your life.

ENTERING INTO CITIZENSHIP

You and I were born into citizenship, and that is the citizenship we had to start with whether we wanted it or not. We were born into both sonship (or daughterhood) and legal citizenship at the same time. Obviously, physical birth is the primary way to become a citizen of a country. You may not be able to drive a car or vote in an election until you reach a certain age, but you will be considered a citizen from day one of your life.

Soon after you learn how to talk, you learn your family name and the name of your country. Soon you will be able to complete the sentence, "I am a citizen of _____." You may not know what that means yet, but you are living it.

You do not have to practice or rehearse being a citizen. I never had to practice to be a Bahamian. ("Today, I'm going to be a Bahamian. I'm going to think hard about it all day....") You also do not have to practice certain rituals as part of your citizenship. No, I became a full Bahamian citizen by virtue of my birth in Bain Town, a humble little place near Freeport on the western end of the island of Grand Bahama. It is my identity, and it is permanent unless I decide to go to a lot of trouble to change it.

Much of what it means to be a citizen will be a natural part of your life. But sometimes you can appreciate and appropriate more of the benefits of your citizenship by thinking about what it means to *enter into* it. Here are a few ways you can enter more fully into the already-full citizenship you possess:

- *Experience* it right now. You do not have to wait until you are older and you do not have to visit the capital city. If you are a citizen living in a colony, you do not have to wait until you can travel to the country that colonized your region. You can experience your citizenship right where you are.

- *Explore* your citizenship. Just becoming a citizen does not mean you know everything about your country or its freedoms and restrictions. If you are a citizen of the United States, you have fifty states and the District of Columbia to explore. You have 300,000 people to meet, different languages to learn, different foods to taste. You could spend the rest of your life exploring your country.

- *Apply* your rights. Lay hold of the benefits and ask for the protections. Enjoy what belongs to you. Being a citizen who does not know his or her rights is like being a non-citizen.

- *Live* in the culture where you are a citizen. Embrace more of it. Live a lifestyle that befits a citizen of your country.

- *Submit* to the constitutional laws and codes of conduct of your nation. Not only will you stay out of trouble, you will reinforce your claim on the rights and benefits that are yours by virtue of your citizenship status.

As part of entering more completely into your precious citizenship, you may decide to take a look at a copy of the constitution of your country, in spite of the fact that its legal terminology may be difficult to comprehend. Most people never do this. Many people do not even think about the fact that their citizenship is controlled by a document called a constitution.

If you are a citizen living in a colony, you do not have to wait until you can travel to the country that colonized your region. You can experience your citizenship right where you are.

Now it's true that people can interpret the same constitution in different ways, but that does not make it powerless. It is also true that the constitution of your country was written by legislators who are more than likely very elderly if not already dead, so nobody can consult them and get the final word about what they intended when they chose the wording. Nevertheless, it is the only constitution you have, unless you claim dual citizenship.

Keep the word "constitution" in mind as you continue to read this book, because I want to make another important point about it later. This is a book about the most special kind of citizenship you can possess, and the attributes of your national citizenship can help you understand your Kingdom citizenship.

CHAPTER 4

THE PRINCIPLE OF DUAL CITIZENSHIP

Over forty nations are represented in my church in Nassau. It is a very international place. When we assemble on a Sunday morning, I can look around the big room and point out many of them—one family from the Philippines, another from Haiti, several people from Jamaica, a good number from various states in the United States, and some who have come to visit or live here from African countries. Each of these citizens of another government arrived in the Bahamas as a guest. Some of them intend to stay and seek Bahamian citizenship, exchanging it for the citizenship they started out with, while others will retain their original citizenship even as they adopt a new one. They will hold dual citizenship.

One of our members works in Florida, which isn't very far away from the Bahamas. He said to me not long ago, "Pastor Myles, I just got my American citizenship." I asked him if he was going to give up his Bahamian citizenship. "No!" he said. "I want the benefits of both countries. The Bahamas is not a poor country. If anything happens to my job in the States, I will come back."

Another young man who visited my congregation is originally from Haiti and he got United States citizenship, too. I congratulated him, and I asked him if he kept his Haitian citizenship. "Nope," he smiled, "I'm an American now." He saw no need to explain why he did not want to keep both citizenships.

In both cases, these men were following the promise of a better life. They moved to a country where the economy was stronger and opportunities for advancement were more numerous. In the new country, they had access to better healthcare and education for their children, and they even liked the climate. One man had left a fairly promising situation for an even more promising one, and the other man decided that his former situation did not have any promise at all. In fact, he no longer cared to be identified with his former country, so he stopped using his Haitian passport. He was not much tempted to go back.

One of the pastors on our staff was born in the United States. His mother is American and his father is Bahamian. So he was born into his American citizenship, but when he grew up he decided to also acquire Bahamian citizenship because of his father, and he moved to live here. He chose to carry dual citizenship. Now he has one leg in each country, and if something bad happens in one country, he can turn to the other one.

Citizenship is not just a piece of paper. Your citizenship represents the entire country.

THROWING DOWN YOUR ANCHOR

Our citizenship should be a source of security, and we all need to be anchored somewhere. If you have no anchor, you drift wherever the current goes and you never achieve very much.

Remember: citizenship is not just a piece of paper. Your citizenship represents the entire country. After all, what do you call yourself as a citizen? You call yourself after the country, don't you? I am a citizen of the Bahamas, so I am a Bahamian. A citizen of the United States of America is an American. A citizen of Nigeria is a Nigerian. Somebody from Bulgaria is a Bulgarian. In a way, you are not just a person anymore—you are a country!

This means that, as I mentioned in chapter 2, a citizen of the Kingdom of Heaven could be called a "heavenling" or a "heavenian," although we do not have a word for it. Two thousand years ago, when people asked Jesus, "Where are you from?" His answer was that He came from Heaven. His point was that he was not from the Earth as they were. He happened to be living on the planet Earth, but his citizenship was in another country, Heaven.

As He explained what He was talking about, people began to understand that He was inviting them to claim heavenly citizenship too. In fact, if they agreed to become "colonists," as I described, they would obtain that heavenly citizenship automatically. At the same time, the only practical thing to do would be to retain their citizenship within a country or kingdom on Earth, because that is where they lived and worked and bore their children. So they would need to carry dual citizenship for the rest of their earthly lives.

That invitation still holds. You and I may be very clear in our minds about what country we belong to. But as we learn about the heavenly kingdom (and how it comes with our heavenly sonship, which we will learn more about later in this book), we too will carry dual citizenship—if not triple citizenship as in the case of my friends who already have two earthly citizenships to their name. You will adapt to overlapping cultures, but you will throw down your anchor in the place where you see the most promise.

STOP MAKING THE EARTH YOUR FIRST REFERENCE

A man named Paul was one of the most vocal expositors of the promises of the Kingdom of God. In the years after the crucifixion of Jesus, he explained the Kingdom of God from one side of the Mediterranean Sea to the other. He wrote a letter to a group of believers in a region that is part of northern Greece today. He was trying to help them deal with persecution from their Roman rulers. The most helpful thing he could tell them was to remind them that they did not need to cope with the persecution by using the same reference points (in other words, conflicts between earthly citizenship rights), because in fact "our citizenship is in heaven" (Phil. 3:20).

The Kingdom economy is never affected by anything, and all the power of Heaven is working in our favor. Your future is secure—and so is your present.

Just like any earthly citizenship, heavenly citizenship is safeguarded. Even if your fellow citizens do not like you, they cannot strip it from you. Under the covering of your heavenly citizenship, you can avoid the contentiousness that comes from the kingdom of darkness and you can steer clear of the bad advice that leads to dead-end solutions. When you learn to make a priority of your Kingdom citizenship, you find yourself in a win-win situation every time.

Dual citizenship is particularly powerful when it is both earthly and divine at the same time. The colonization effort of the Kingdom God is designed to bring Kingdom citizens the advantage of dual citizenship, because the earthly citizenship we start out with cannot protect us.

If only we could learn to stop making our earthly citizenship our first reference! The Kingdom economy is never affected by anything, and all the power of Heaven is working in our favor. Your future is secure—and so is your present. None of it depends on what happens in this world, good or bad, only on what happens in Heaven. And in Heaven, everything is always okay.

From chapter 1, remember what I said about the kingdom of darkness and the kingdom of light. The whole reason I wanted to bring up the idea of dual citizenship is because if you choose to become a citizen of the Kingdom of Heaven, inevitably you will hold dual citizenship, whether or not you recognize the fact. All earthly citizenships, even the ones that supply excellent benefits and protections, are tainted by the kingdom of darkness. How could it be otherwise? But once you hold dual citizenship, you can give preference to the kingdom of light, and I guarantee that you will not regret it.

Most Christians are not in the Kingdom. I know that is a shocking statement. Members of other religions are not either.

That is because most people who identify themselves as members of a Christian church have remained *citizens* of the same kingdom of darkness as the people around them. As such, they can only rise to the level of the jurisdiction under which they live. Their lifestyle does not change. They may attend meetings at a church, but they are not as "born again" as they may think they are. Just watch: sing on Sunday and cuss on Monday. That's the way it goes.

They do not carry dual citizenship. They cannot give preference to a superior citizenship, because they do not know about it and they have not sought it out. They do not reflect the culture of the Kingdom, which is a culture of light, freedom from conflict, and more.

TIME TO PAY YOUR DUES

Citizenship in the Kingdom immerses you in a culture, not a collection of rituals. That is hard to get across, because we were born into a collection of rituals. Every organized religion, even the simplest ones, have them. They have meetings and procedures and programs and customs and fees; it is all worked out. Every weekend the religions crank up their rituals. (Most of the Christians hold their meetings on Sundays. The Seventh-Day Adventists and the Jews hold theirs on Saturdays. The Muslims hold theirs on Fridays. Everybody's got their special days.)

Citizenship in the Kingdom immerses you in a culture, not a collection of rituals.

I mentioned in chapter 3 that you cannot "practice" citizenship. The word has a double meaning. Not only can you not practice and rehearse for citizenship, you cannot claim citizenship because you practice and perform various rituals. You can practice a performance or a religion, but never citizenship.

You cannot "do" a country like you do a ritual. Think about it. How many times are you a citizen? At what time of day? For how long? Only on the weekend for an hour? Only when you are using a certain language or eating certain foods?

You just *are* a citizen, aren't you? If all the lights go out, you are still a citizen. If you do not pay your taxes or your tithes, you are still a citizen. You may be an irresponsible citizen, but you are still a citizen no matter where you go. And if you are a kingdom citizen in good standing with your king, you will go far.

THE KINGDOM IS WITHIN YOU

I have found that the Bible explains everything better than I can explain it. Here is a good place to pull out a few lines to explain how the culture of Kingdom citizenship is completely different from any other culture:

> *Now when He was asked by the Pharisees when the kingdom of God would come, He answered them and said, "The kingdom of God does not come with observation; nor will they say, 'See here!' or 'See there!' For indeed, the kingdom of God is within you." (Luke 17:20-21)*

> *The wind blows where it wishes, and you hear the sound of it, but cannot tell where it comes from and where it goes. So is everyone who is born of the Spirit. (John 3:8)*

When they are talking about the Kingdom, people do not say, "There it is, over there!" They can't say that because, like any citizenship, it is invisible, although it makes a noticeable difference in its citizens. It is incorporated inside of its citizens.

The Kingdom of God does not wear a sign.

People can detect a certain essence of its presence, but it is almost like noticing the way the wind shakes a leaf. To a new citizen of the Kingdom, they may say, "Hey, what is different about you? You don't go with us to the club anymore until the wee hours. You carry yourself differently. You even drive differently. What happened to you? They didn't see anything happen. What can you say? "Uh, I had an encounter with another country and my priorities changed." This Kingdom causes you to rearrange the furniture inside you, and you do not want to put it back the way it used to be. You become almost like a country within a country—a dual citizen, for a fact.

Every time I go to Los Angeles, I always ask my host to please take me to Chinatown because I like Chinese food. You enter Chinatown through an amazing gate with a dragon on it. Once you drive through the gate, it is as though you are in China. The signs are in Chinese. The people are Chinese. The conversation is conducted in Chinese. You would never go there for pizza, and you would not ask for directions to the nearest McDonald's. When you go to Chinatown, you know what to expect, and you do not expect it to be the same as the rest of the American city outside the gate.

As a citizen of the Kingdom you should be distinctive in a similar way. You begin to forget how to speak the same language as the country you used to be part of. That is why your old friends know they can't use dirty words around you anymore, or gossip, or persuade you to tell a lie. Something has changed, and it is your citizenship. After a while, the people around you will learn what to expect.

When we become citizens of the Kingdom of Heaven, we have some learning—and un-learning—to do. We have been away from Home so long we think we are earthlings and we have picked up an earthly culture.

Another way of saying the words quoted above would be to say, "The Kingdom of God does not wear a sign." That's the way it is with citizenship. How do people know I am a Bahamian? How do they know you are a South African? We don't wear T-shirts that say so, do we? We don't wear baseball caps with our national insignia on them and we don't wear tags that announce, "American citizen." Citizenship is not easily observable. It can be hard to detect. Sometimes people can't tell until you open your mouth, and a lot of times they can't tell even from your language or your accent.

GETTING THE CULTURE BACK

When we are away from home for a long time, living in another country, we pick up the local culture. When we return home, people can figure out that we have been someplace else. We have picked up vocabulary that we did not used to have, and our daily routines have changed.

The same thing happens when you join the Army or any of the armed services. As long as you are part of the armed forces, you are not considered a civilian. You must follow a stringent set of rules, even down to what kind of belt or shoes you wear. If your commanding officer says "Jump!" you jump. People who return to civilian life after a long stretch in the military sometimes have an adjustment problem. Outside, everything is different. Inside, they still feel like they are living within the gates of the military complex.

When we become citizens of the Kingdom of Heaven, we have some learning—and un-learning—to do. We have been away from Home so long we think we are earthlings and we have picked up an earthly culture. That is one of the biggest reasons Kingdom citizens need to pray, "Thy Kingdom come, Thy will be done, on earth as it is in Heaven," for the sake of getting their own culture back, if for nothing else. Kingdom citizens need to re-educate themselves to think like heavenly citizens, because they've almost forgotten how.

As a matter of fact, a Kingdom citizen is one of Heaven's reps, and he or she needs to represent that country everyplace. Kingdom citizenship has been conferred upon them. The Son of the King explained it like this: "I confer on you a kingdom, just as my Father conferred one on me" (Luke 22:29, NIV). As a Kingdom citizen, not only do you represent the culture, you carry the King's authority with you. This makes a big difference in the way you conduct yourself. A whole country has been conferred upon you.

That means that when you go to work in the morning, Heaven comes with you. Heaven drives your car down the highway. Heaven stops at a gas station to buy fuel. How does Heaven act under pressure? If someone cuts you off in traffic, how does Heaven respond?

These are the real issues of citizenship, and you will deal with them every day. Do you represent your country properly? Representing your country is part of your corporate responsibility. People will be watching you, and because of you, they will decide what they think of the King and His Kingdom. You want to make sure that you have not been away from home for so long (so to speak) that you have picked up the local culture.

People who are from earth have their minds on earthly things. (This fact is noted in Philippians 3:19.) Their minds reflect the culture around them, and they can't help it. They try to solve their problems from the perspective of the people and culture around them. They do not have the advantage of calling on the wisdom and stability and wealth of the Kingdom of Heaven. They do not even know that it is an option.

Representing your country is part of your corporate responsibility. People will be watching you, and because of you, they will decide what they think of the King and His Kingdom.

WHAT IS YOUR CONTINGENCY PLAN?

I told you about my friends who have dual citizenship. With dual citizenship, they have a contingency plan. If things do not work out in the country on one side of the ocean, they can move back to the other country.

You do not want to live as if you have declared independence from Heaven. You want to hang onto the dual citizenship, and you want to give preference to it regardless of what continent or island you may be living on. The currency of the Kingdom of Heaven can be used in any country on the face of the earth, because it is called love. The educational system keeps you on top of things at all times, because you never stop learning. The social service system is so good it is beyond description.

I made my citizenship in that Kingdom my first choice a long time ago, and I hope you do, too. I assure you that you will never find a better kind of citizenship anywhere. Keep reading to find out how to become a citizen of the Kingdom of Heaven, if you are not already one, and how to enjoy fully the privileges and advantages of that citizenship wherever you may go on this Earth.

CHAPTER 5

THE UNIQUENESS OF KINGDOM CITIZENSHIP

Everybody in the world knows what Jesus did two thousand years ago, even the pagans. The atheists know what He did. The Muslims and the Hindus know, too, whether they believe it or not. When Jesus died on that bloody Roman cross outside the city of Jerusalem, crucified, His death rocked the foundations of human culture so deeply that they have never stopped reverberating.

His death is so well-known because He did not stay dead for long. You cannot kill the King of Heaven, as people discovered when He rose from the dead after only three days in the grave. As a matter of fact, this King happens to be the most unique king in human history, because He is still alive, and His Kingdom is, too.

EXAMINING THE EVIDENCE

Although everybody knows what Jesus did, relatively few people—and this includes Christians, the ones who talk the most about Jesus—know what He stands for. They have not perceived the fact that when Jesus was working and teaching in Jerusalem and in the towns all up and down the countryside, His primary message was about the Kingdom of Heaven, which was His home country. He talked about the Kingdom all the time, using that very term.

Somebody counted how many times the word "kingdom" is mentioned in the New Testament of the Bible (the part that was written after Jesus was born), and they found it about 162 times. Most of these times, "kingdom" is referring to the Kingdom of God.

The four books written by Jesus' disciples Matthew, Mark, Luke and John are known as the Gospels, and they contain the firsthand accounts of the events of Jesus' life. The Gospel of Matthew uses the phrase "Kingdom of Heaven." The authors of the other three Gospels prefer "Kingdom of God." The two terms mean the same thing.

When Jesus was working and teaching in Jerusalem and in the towns all up and down the countryside, His primary message was about the Kingdom of Heaven, which was His home country.

So all through Jesus' recorded preaching, the word "kingdom" appears far more often than the other words you might expect to see, such as "eternal life," "born again," "forgiveness," or "love." Jesus talked about the Kingdom all the time. It was His main topic, His primary reference point. In fact, you would be exactly right if you said that Jesus' whole purpose in coming to Earth was to reintroduce the Kingdom of Heaven to a world that had completely lost track of the truth about it.

SON OF THE KING, SON OF MAN

You could say that Jesus Christ is the most misunderstood person on the Earth, because even His closest followers, the Christians (who people who carry His name), have misconstrued His message. I would go so far as to call it a tragedy that we have produced a religion called Christianity. Jesus Christ did not invent such a thing. Even in the Bible stories about Him and about the undertakings of His disciples, the word "Christian" is used only twice, and one of them is derogatory.

It is time to set things straight. Jesus did not come to set up a religion. He came to establish an outpost of the Kingdom of Heaven.

Jesus did not exercise his right to become a teacher until he was thirty years old. Then for the next three years, He roamed the countryside as an itinerant rabbi, teaching anyone who would listen what the Kingdom was like and demonstrating its liberating power with miraculous signs.

A good part of His message was "repent"—change your thinking. Change your thinking to what? To Kingdom thinking, to a recognition of heavenly lordship. That is what He said in the first recorded words of his teaching:

> From that time [immediately after His baptism and forty days in the wilderness] Jesus began to preach and to say, "Repent, for the kingdom of heaven is at hand." (Matt. 4:17)

From that time on Jesus began to preach, "Repent, for the kingdom of heaven has come near." (Matt. 4:17, NIV)

The words "at hand" and "near" mean the same thing. The Kingdom was approaching, and Jesus was announcing its coming. As a matter of fact, He was ushering it in.

He did not give people more laws and religious rituals to learn. They had enough of those already. He wanted to tell people what to do with their lives, how to become naturalized (perhaps I should say "supernaturalized") citizens of the Kingdom of Heaven.

> *Jesus did not come to set up a religion. He came to establish an outpost of the Kingdom of Heaven.*

After He spent three years teaching, preaching, and demonstrating what the Kingdom was like, some people objected to His ideas so much that they plotted to have him killed. You would think that would have taken care of it. Dead men can't preach against your cherished religion and a man in a tomb can no longer claim to be leading the way to this so-called Kingdom. His opponents especially disliked the fact that He seemed to be claiming some kind of kingship.

Yet as we know now, even His bloody crucifixion failed to defeat the Kingdom. In fact, Jesus' death and subsequent resurrection completed the purpose of His mission to earth—to re-establish a Kingdom outpost among the people who lived under the human jurisdictions of the world, to reclaim the territory of Earth for the Kingdom of Heaven.

OUTPOST OF THE KINGDOM OF HEAVEN

Originally, the Kingdom of Heaven had established an outpost in a place that people know as the Garden of Eden. Here is how the first book of the Bible describes it:

> *Then God said, "Let Us make man in Our image, according to Our likeness; let them have dominion over the fish of the sea, over the birds of the air, and over the cattle, over all the earth and over every creeping thing that creeps on the earth." So God created man in His own image; in the image of God He created him; male and female He created them.* (Gen. 1:26-27)

"Let them have dominion," God said. The word used in the original Hebrew is *mamlakah*. This word *mamlakah* turns out to be the same word that gets translated into English as "kingdom." It also gets translated as "reign," "sovereignty," and "realm." So dominion is the same as kingdom. You can see the "dom" syllable in both words because the words "dominion" and "kingdom" are closely related.

All of these words indicate that someone is in charge of something. Having dominion means having authority over. It means leading, managing, ruling over. According to the account in Genesis, human beings were created to manage the rest of Creation. We can see this throughout the rest of the story about the first man and woman, and on through all of human history up to the present day.

"Let them have dominion." The King was assigning dominion to the people He had created. What were the people supposed to have dominion over? Their assignment on earth was to manage the real estate He had created as an extension of His rule in Heaven. First He created the earth and all the living things that fill it, and then the King brought Heaven to earth and set up His government, His system of management.

God created the humans with the intention of having them represent His authority on the planet He had created.

MANAGEMENT FAILURE

We call the first man and woman Adam and Eve. How did they do with their assignment? Not very well. Here's their part of the story:

> *Then the Lord God took the man and put him in the garden of Eden to tend and keep it. And the Lord God commanded the man, saying, "Of every tree of the garden you may freely eat; but of the tree of the knowledge of good and evil you shall not eat, for in the day that you eat of it you shall surely die."* (Gen. 2:15-17)

As managers of the outpost of the Kingdom of Heaven, they had only one restriction: do not eat the fruit from that particular tree. That one rule was evidently very important to God, because He told them that breaking it would mean death. But a wily serpent came along and contradicted what God had said. Adam's wife Eve believed the serpent's lie, and she took a bite, offering some to her husband as well. God confronted them:

> Then to Adam He said, "Because you have heeded the voice of your wife, and have eaten from the tree of which I commanded you, saying, 'You shall not eat of it':
>
> "Cursed is the ground for your sake;
>
> In toil you shall eat of it
>
> All the days of your life.
>
> Both thorns and thistles it shall bring forth for you,
>
> And you shall eat the herb of the field.
>
> In the sweat of your face you shall eat bread
>
> Till you return to the ground,
>
> For out of it you were taken;
>
> For dust you are,
>
> And to dust you shall return."
>
> ...Therefore the Lord God sent him out of the garden of Eden to till the ground from which he was taken. So He drove out the man.... (Gen. 3:17-19, 23-24)

No longer could the Kingdom of Heaven claim to have an outpost on the Earth. God had created the humans with the intention of having them represent His authority on the planet He had created. He had wanted them to exercise dominion for Him. They failed. We call it the Fall. This is the declaration of independence that I described in the second chapter of this book. The colonists had ruptured their relationship with their King, and they could not repair it. The only way the colony could be re-established would have to involve the King's Son.

Most people do not understand that Jesus makes it possible for them to re-engage with God's original plan. They know next to nothing about becoming citizens of the Kingdom and very little about resuming their role as God's representatives in the territory called Earth.

THE KING'S SON

The name of the King's Son was, of course, Jesus. He did not come to Earth for a long time. Many generations of people lived and died in the meantime. Some of them began to expect Him someday. Religious people talked about it. In the whole region not far from where the first man had failed to manage the first colony of the Kingdom, prophets would try to describe what God was going to do. Some of them got very specific:

> *For unto us a Child is born,*
> *Unto us a Son is given;*
> *And the government will be upon His shoulder.*
> *And His name will be called*
> *Wonderful, Counselor, Mighty God,*
> *Everlasting Father, Prince of Peace.*
> *Of the increase of His government and peace*
> *There will be no end....* (Isa. 9:6-7)

This Child that the prophet Isaiah was talking about was coming to re-establish the government of Heaven on the Earth.

He would *not* be coming to set up a better religion, because Adam hadn't lost a religion; he had lost dominion.

When the Son finally did arrive, most people did not know who He was. They thought He was the firstborn son of a simple carpenter and his wife. They did not understand until later that He was the long-expected Son of God, the "Second Adam," whose life, death, and resurrection would undo the judgment that had been rendered upon Adam so long before. Even to this day, in spite of centuries of the religion called Christianity, most people do not understand that Jesus makes it possible for them to re-engage with God's original plan. They know next to nothing about becoming citizens of the Kingdom Jesus talked so much about, and very little about resuming their role as God's representatives in the territory called Earth.

HOW JESUS TALKED ABOUT THE KINGDOM

The New Testament documents Jesus' message about this most unique Kingdom. Here are just some of the very many times He talked about the Kingdom. Many of these passages may be familiar to you. The quotations marks indicate that Jesus is speaking. I have highlighted the word "kingdom" throughout:

> *"The Law and the Prophets were proclaimed until John. Since that time, the good news of the **kingdom** of God is being preached, and everyone is forcing their way into it." (Luke 16:16, NIV)*

> *Jesus said, "My **kingdom** is not of this world. If it were, my servants would fight to prevent my arrest by the Jewish leaders. But now my **kingdom** is from another place." (John 18:36, NIV)*

*"Do not worry about your life, what you will eat or what you will drink; nor about your body, what you will put on...Seek first the **kingdom** of God and His righteousness, and all these things shall be added to you"* (Matt. 6:25,33).

*And Jesus went about all Galilee, teaching in their synagogues, preaching the gospel of the **kingdom**, and healing all kinds of sickness and all kinds of disease among the people.* (Matt. 4:23)

*At daybreak, Jesus went out to a solitary place. The people were looking for him and when they came to where he was, they tried to keep him from leaving them. But he said, "I must proclaim the good news of the **kingdom** of God to the other towns also, because that is why I was sent."* (Luke 4:42-43, NIV)

*These twelve Jesus sent out and commanded them... "And as you go, preach, saying, 'The **kingdom** of heaven is at hand.'"* (Matt. 10:5,7)

*"I will give you the keys of the **kingdom** of heaven; whatever you bind on earth will be bound in heaven, and whatever you loose on earth will be loosed in heaven."* (Matt. 16:19, NIV)

*"Truly I tell you, some who are standing here will not taste death before they see the Son of Man coming in his **kingdom**."* (Matt. 16:28, NIV)

"In this manner, therefore, pray:
Our Father in heaven,
Hallowed be Your name.

*Your **kingdom** come.*

Your will be done

On earth as it is in heaven.

Give us this day our daily bread.

And forgive us our debts,

As we forgive our debtors.

And do not lead us into temptation,

But deliver us from the evil one.

*For Yours is the **kingdom** and the power and the glory forever. Amen."* (Matt. 6:9-13)

*"And this gospel of the **kingdom** will be preached in the whole world as a testimony to all nations, and then the end will come."* (Matt. 24:14, NIV)

*"When anyone hears the message about the **kingdom** and does not understand it, the evil one comes and snatches away what was sown in their heart."* (Matt. 13:19, NIV)

*Another parable He put forth to them, saying: "The **kingdom** of heaven is like a mustard seed, which a man took and sowed in his field, which indeed is the least of all the seeds; but when it is grown it is greater than the herbs and becomes a tree, so that the birds of the air come and nest in its branches."* (Matt. 13:31-32)

*Another parable He spoke to them: "The **kingdom** of heaven is like leaven, which a woman took and hid in three measures of meal till it was all leavened."* (Matt. 13:33)

*"Again, the **kingdom** of heaven is like treasure hidden in a field, which a man found and hid; and for joy over it he goes and sells all that he has and buys that field."* (Matt. 13:44)

*"Again, the **kingdom** of heaven is like a merchant seeking beautiful pearls, who, when he had found one pearl of great price, went and sold all that he had and bought it."* (Matt. 13:45-46)

*"Again, the **kingdom** of heaven is like a dragnet that was cast into the sea and gathered some of every kind, which, when it was full, they drew to shore; and they sat down and gathered the good into vessels, but threw the bad away."* (Matt. 13:47-48)

And seeing the multitudes, He went up on a mountain, and when He was seated His disciples came to Him. Then He opened His mouth and taught them, saying:
"Blessed are the poor in spirit,
*For theirs is the **kingdom** of heaven....*
Blessed are those who are persecuted for righteousness' sake,
*For theirs is the **kingdom** of heaven."* (Matt. 5:1-3,10)

*Once, on being asked by the Pharisees when the **kingdom** of God would come, Jesus replied, "The coming of the **kingdom** of God is not something that can be observed, nor will people say, 'Here it is,' or 'There it is,' because the **kingdom** of God is in your midst."* (Luke 17:20-21, NIV)

Jesus even kept talking about the Kingdom after He rose from the grave:

> *After his suffering, he presented himself to them and gave many convincing proofs that he was alive. He appeared to them over a period of forty days and spoke about the **kingdom** of God.* (Acts 1:3, NIV)

Jesus never stopped talking about the Kingdom. He was careful about referring to Himself as the King, and yet His disciples could tell that He was the one that all of the prophets from Joshua to Malachi had been talking about when they announced the coming of a future Messiah. Some of the books in the Old Testament had given details about his lineage (such as the book of Ruth, for example). Others proclaimed the future coming of an unnamed, magnificent king who would take care of all the injustices that plagued the nation of Israel. Psalmists such as King David provided tantalizing details (see Psalms 22 and 45). The prophet Micah included the name of the village in which Jesus' mother Mary would give birth to Him:

> *But you, Bethlehem Ephrathah,*
> *Though you are little among the thousands of Judah,*
> *Yet out of you shall come forth to Me*
> *The One to be Ruler in Israel,*
> *Whose goings forth are from of old,*
> *From everlasting.* (Mic. 5:2)

In the very beginning, the Father had said "Let us make man in our own image and let them have dominion over the earth," and He never changed His mind. God fitted you as a human being to have dominion over the earth, to steward its resources, to allow yourself to be directed by His will. Every one of us fell away, however, because Adam and Eve did, and we needed to be restored to our intended position of rulership and dominion in the context of a heavenly Kingdom. We could never restore ourselves to Kingdom citizenship again on our own, because the situation is beyond our capabilities. So the Father sent His Son Jesus to restore Heaven's government and to repair what Adam had destroyed. As that first man had lost the heavenly assignment for the whole race, the "Second Adam," Jesus, restored it. Now all we have to do is to recognize what He has done and get on board.

Jesus never stopped talking about the Kingdom.

HOW OTHERS TALKED ABOUT JESUS' COMING KINGDOM

Not only did Jesus talk unceasingly about the Kingdom, His disciples and others did as well. John (the one we call John the Baptist because he baptized a lot of people, including Jesus) was Jesus' cousin. He started talking about the Kingdom before Jesus became known to the public. His was a prophetic voice and he is considered a "forerunner" of Jesus:

> *In those days John the Baptist came, preaching in the wilderness of Judea and saying,* ***"Repent, for the kingdom of heaven has come near."*** *This is he who was spoken of through the prophet Isaiah:*
>
> *"A voice of one calling in the wilderness,*

'Prepare the way for the Lord,

make straight paths for him.'" (Matt. 3:1-3, NIV, emphasis mine)

Jesus sent out his first twelve disciples to talk about what it means to be citizens in His Kingdom, and they in turn commissioned all of His other followers to do the same, wherever their paths took them. We do not have a written record of what most them said, but here are a few examples, again with the key word emphasized:

*But when they believed Philip as he preached the things concerning the **kingdom of God** and the name of Jesus Christ, both men and women were baptized.* (Acts 8:12)

*And when they had preached the gospel to that city and made many disciples, they returned to Lystra, Iconium, and Antioch, strengthening the souls of the disciples, exhorting them to continue in the faith, and saying, "We must through many tribulations enter the **kingdom of God**." So when they had appointed elders in every church, and prayed with fasting, they commended them to the Lord in whom they had believed.* (Acts 14:21-23)

*Listen, my beloved brethren: Has God not chosen the poor of this world to be rich in faith and heirs of the **kingdom** which He promised to those who love Him?* (James. 2:5)

Therefore, my brothers and sisters, make every effort to confirm your calling and election. For if you do these things, you will never stumble, and you will *receive a rich welcome into the **eternal kingdom** of our Lord and Savior Jesus Christ.* (2 Pet. 1:10-12, NIV)

Paul was so determined to talk about the Kingdom that he once suspended his travels for more than two years in order to talk about it.

Paul travelled more than all of them, and he talked about the Kingdom when he wrote letters to the believers all across the Mediterranean world:

*The **kingdom of God** is not eating and drinking, but righteousness and peace and joy in the Holy Spirit.* (Rom. 14:17, emphasis mine)

*Some of you have become arrogant, as if I were not coming to you. But I will come to you very soon, if the Lord is willing, and then I will find out not only how these arrogant people are talking, but what power they have. For the **kingdom of God** is not a matter of talk but of power* (1 Cor. 4:18-20, NIV, emphasis mine)

*For **our citizenship is in heaven**, from which we also eagerly wait for the Savior, the Lord Jesus Christ.* (Phil. 3:20, emphasis mine)

In fact, Paul was so determined to talk about the Kingdom that he once suspended his travels for more than two years in order to talk about it. He was in Ephesus at the time:

Paul entered the synagogue and spoke boldly there for three months, arguing persuasively about the kingdom of God. But some of them became obstinate; they refused to believe and publicly maligned the Way. So Paul left them. He took the disciples with him and had discussions daily in the lecture hall of Tyrannus. This went on for two years.... (Acts 19:8-10, NIV)

Before this, Paul had always moved on to a new city. He actually stopped traveling for two years in order to stay in the same city and get the Kingdom into the hearts and minds of the people. Remember, the Kingdom is a country. You can't explain everything about it in thirty minutes. You can't explain everything about the country where you live in that length of time, either. Paul could not teach enough about the Kingdom in one sitting. He talked about it for several hours every single day for two years! He was describing the country of Heaven and how it affects the people on Earth. He talked about colonizing the known world, and about importing the Kingdom constitution and all of its laws, along with the intricacies of social relations and cultural expressions.

We must learn about the Kingdom and we must become citizens as soon as we can.

At the end of his life, Paul restated the fact that he, like Jesus, had preached about one topic, the Kingdom of God:

*And indeed, now I know that you all, among whom
I have gone preaching the kingdom of God, will see
my face no more.* (Acts 20:25)

Paul was taken to Rome as a prisoner. A long time passed
before he went to trial. What did he do with his time? He
taught about the Kingdom, of course:

*So when they had appointed him a day, many came
to him at his lodging, to whom he explained and
solemnly testified of the kingdom of God, persuading
them concerning Jesus from both the Law of Moses
and the Prophets, from morning till evening.* (Acts
28:23)

*Then Paul dwelt two whole years in his own rented
house, and received all who came to him, preaching
the kingdom of God and teaching the things which
concern the Lord Jesus Christ with all confidence, no
one forbidding him.* (Acts 28: 30-31)

Any subject that so dominates the preaching and teaching
in the Bible must be worth our entire attention. We must learn
about the Kingdom and we must become citizens as soon as
we can.

THE IMPORTANCE OF BECOMING
A KINGDOM CITIZEN

I will put it to you: the Kingdom is the secret to life. The
secret to a full and fulfilled life is the discovery, understanding,
and application of the Kingdom of Heaven on earth. You have
to learn how the Kingdom works, how to apply what you have
learned every day. Religion will make you keep postponing the

Kingdom until the future, by and by when you die. It is time to start living in the Kingdom here and now. Chapter 9 will describe how to become a citizen of this kingdom (or how to know if you are already one).

The Kingdom of God is now. You must enter into citizenship while you are still on earth. You cannot appropriate what you keep postponing. You can never experience what you keep putting off. You will never be able to enjoy what you believe is not here yet. Living in the Kingdom is a daily activity, now. Today, I live Kingdom life. Today I am a citizen, and I experience the full rights and responsibilities of citizenship.

The Kingdom of God is now. You must enter into citizenship while you are still on earth.

No religion or ritual can substitute for the Kingdom. The Kingdom is what you are looking for. Your religion isn't enough. The Kingdom of Heaven is like that "pearl of great price" or the treasure hidden in the field that Jesus talked about—something so precious that the one who finds it rushes out to sell everything he owns in order to buy it.

The man who found the treasure and the man who found the pearl sold everything. In the same way, we need to sell everything in order to be "sold out" for the Kingdom. We need to sell all of our old belief systems and previous opinions. Some of us need to sell our theological degrees for the Kingdom. Others need to sell their grandmother's denomination, into which they were born. Some need to sell their loyalty to the pastor they love so much but who isn't preaching about the Kingdom. Everything you have valued needs to go because all of it pales in comparison to the treasured pearl of the Kingdom.

As a Christian, you may think you have already got the pearl—until you find the real thing. Humans are collecting all kinds of pearls, searching for the best one. Some choose Islam; that is a pearl. Some choose Buddhism; that is a pearl. Some choose Mormonism. Some choose yoga. Some choose Unitarianism. Some choose atheism. All of those are pearls. And the minute a person discovers the Kingdom, which is not a religion even though it may carry the name of Jesus Christ, they know they have found all that they ever wanted. They can give up all of the other pearls.

As a Christian, you may still worry about tomorrow and fret about the present. As a Kingdom citizen, you can count on the limitless resources of your heavenly Father as never before. You may need to learn some things about being a Kingdom citizen before you can enjoy those resources, but they will be yours for the asking. "It is your Father's good pleasure to give you the kingdom" (Luke 12:32).

THE BIBLE AS THE CONSTITUTION OF THE KINGDOM

A king's will, purpose, and intent are expressed in the form of laws. Any country has laws, and the Kingdom of Heaven is no exception. The Bible is filled with the laws of God, and that means we can call it the constitution of the Kingdom of God.

When you read the Bible, you come away with a strong impression of "Thy will be done." We call the older part of the Bible the "Old Testament" and the newer part the "New Testament." A testament is simply a documented will, God's will in this case. (Your "last will and testament" is your documented statement about how you wish to distribute your possessions upon death.) The collection of books we call the Bible is filled with the King's ideas and promises about His own country and what He wants for His own citizens. It is God's testament.

The Bible, filled with God's thoughts, is the constitution of the Kingdom. It is not subject to change.

In a democracy, a constitution comes from the people. In fact, in the United States of America, the first words of the constitution are "We, the people...." The constitution of the Bahamas begins in a similar way. But when a constitution comes from "we, the people," it can be changed by the people.

In a kingdom, the constitution comes straight from the head of the king. His thoughts become the constitution. The Bible, filled with God's thoughts, is the constitution of the Kingdom. It is not subject to change.

The Bible is not only the constitution of the Kingdom, it is God's will—it shows us what our inheritance consists of. One of the most unique things about the Kingdom of Heaven is that the citizens of that Kingdom inherit everything in it. That is not the case with other countries. As a Bahamian, I do not own all the land in the country and I do not possess all the money in the treasury. But in this Kingdom common-wealth, it is different. The wealth is truly held in common. Citizens of the Kingdom of God have inherited it and it belongs to them. Each and every one can lay hold of whatever they need, whenever they need it. The treasury keys are already in their hands.

The Kingdom of God is not a religion, but an authority structure. It is a country with a government, and we live in an outpost of it, a colony.

"I'M FROM THE KINGDOM COUNTRY"

To repeat, the Kingdom of God is not a religion, but an authority structure. It is a country, a country with a government. It may be invisible to our human eyes, but it is a country just the same, and we live in an outpost of it, a colony. When people ask you, "What country are you from?" you can answer, "I'm from the Kingdom country." You may claim dual citizenship as we discussed in chapter 4, but you will want to give the Kingdom country priority over the other country where you have citizenship.

The Kingdom of God—the most unique Kingdom of all. Like Paul and the others whose words are recorded in the Bible, it is all I want to talk about. Read on to explore it further with me.

CHAPTER 6

THE NEED FOR CITIZENS' ORIENTATION

Having just presented the idea that the Bible is the constitution of the Kingdom of God, I want to quote a few statements from that constitution, for the sake of your orientation and alignment with the Kingdom way of doing things. These statements will start to move you into a thought process. The more you read the constitution of the Kingdom with a "Kingdom filter" on your mind, the more the light of understanding will dawn for you. (In the style of legal documents, I will use "sections" and "articles" in place of chapter and verse:)

> *Now, therefore, you are no longer strangers and foreigners, but fellow citizens with the saints and members of the household of God. (Section Ephesians, subsection 2, article 19)*

> *For this reason we also, since the day we heard it, do not cease to pray for you, and to ask that you may be filled with the knowledge of His will in all*

wisdom and spiritual understanding; that you may walk worthy of the Lord, fully pleasing Him, being fruitful in every good work and increasing in the knowledge of God; strengthened with all might, according to His glorious power, for all patience and longsuffering with joy; giving thanks to the Father who has qualified us to be partakers of the inheritance of the saints in the light. (Section Colossians, subsection one, articles 9 through 12)

For our citizenship is in heaven, from which we also eagerly wait for the Savior, the Lord Jesus Christ... (Section Philippians, subsection 3, article 20)

These words in the constitution of the Kingdom were written to citizens of the Kingdom in the present tense. These rights, privileges, and duties belong to every citizen.

These words in the constitution of the Kingdom were written to citizens of the Kingdom in the present tense. They explain some of the current and ongoing rights, privileges, and duties that come with Kingdom citizenship. These rights, privileges, and duties belong to every citizen, including you, even if you are a very new citizen. You cannot earn them or improve on them. You can, however, remain ignorant of them and ignore them. That is why it is so important to talk about the Kingdom and to keep reading its constitution in depth in order to understand it.

Many sections of the Kingdom constitution were written by a citizen named Paul. Paul spent most of his adult life preaching, teaching, and writing letters to citizens of the Kingdom, helping them adjust to the Kingdom lifestyle. Sometimes he had to correct misunderstandings about theological ideas. Yet he was never inventing anything new or establishing a new gospel. He was always addressing Kingdom issues.

This is because the citizens were always having adjustment problems. They had social problems, cultural problems, relationship problems, money problems—every category of problem you can think of. Paul explained to them, "Look, to live in this Kingdom there are some things you need to do, and some other things you need to stop doing, and here they are."

You and I have adjustment problems as well. I am glad Paul wrote as much as he did, because today we can use all the help we can get. We need to understand more about our citizenship in the Kingdom.

Turn your thoughts over to the Creator who made you. Let Him reorient your thinking. He is your King, and He owns it all anyway.

MENTAL TRANSFORMATION

Most of our problems start in our heads. Therefore, we need a mental transformation if we want to become full citizens of the Kingdom. We need to figure out our misconceptions and how to get rid of them, especially those religious concepts that we have been hearing all our lives. You and I want to be citizens of the Kingdom, free from labels and assumptions. I do not want to be Baptist, Methodist, Episcopalian, Catholic, Seventh-Day Adventist, Church of God, Assemblies of God, charismatic, or Pentecostal anymore. I do not want to think of myself as a businessman, a pastor, an advisor, or any other kind of career person. I want misconceptions to be carefully and continually cleaned out of me so I can start over. I want to start fresh as a citizen of the Kingdom of God, and I want you to be able to start fresh, too, looking for the next assignment He will give you.

Turn your thoughts over to the Creator who made you. Let Him reorient your thinking. Turn over all of your possessions to Him. He is your King, and He owns it all anyway. Let Him show you how to redistribute everything you thought you owned.

If you build your whole life on a certain idea and it becomes theory and then philosophy and then doctrine and then a belief system and finally a way of life and a mentality, you will not know that you have basically built your life on a lie.

CORRECT CONCEPTS

Anybody who has studied communications knows what I mean when I say "noise." A sender sends a message to an intended receiver, and noise is what happens during the transmission, in between when the message leaves the sender and gets received by the recipient. The noise can be very complicated to understand because it includes your culture, your educational level, your social upbringing, your religious history, your values, your moral status, and your present situation in life.

For something that is called "noise," a lot of it is very hidden and silent. The most important part of the noise is what I call concepts. A concept is an idea, a thought that has been conceived as a mental picture. Thoughts are very powerful, even the ones that are never expressed in words. (A word is an exposed thought, but most thoughts never get expressed.)

We think first, then we speak or write. We try to express our thoughts and we want others to understand them—but their own thoughts often alter their comprehension, resulting in misunderstandings or misconceptions.

Nothing is as dangerous as a misconception. Marriages can break up because of them. A husband and wife may actually love one another, but misconceptions arise and they enter into conflict. Governments and churches break up because of misconceptions, too. If you build your whole life on a certain idea and it becomes theory and then philosophy and then doctrine and then a belief system and finally a way of life and a mentality, you will not know that you have basically built your life on a lie. To you, it is not a lie; it's the truth, and you will strongly defend even your misconception.

When it comes to truth about you and God, most likely much of what you believe has been contaminated. People interpret words about God through their pre-existing concepts. This includes the words in the Bible. Your seminary degree could be contaminated with ignorance of the true concepts about

God. You and your pastor and your church friends could all have pieces of the truth, but none of you has asked the original Sender to clear your mind of contaminated concepts so you can get the message right.

The King anticipated this problem. This is why He provided an expert Counselor for us—the Holy Spirit—who can personally help you capture the correct concepts that come to you from the mind of God. "He will guide you into all truth," said Jesus' disciple John (John 16:13).

Correct concepts about God include truth about the Kingdom of God. When you rediscover the truth about your Kingdom citizenship, you rediscover something that has been lost over the years. The average person living in the Western world has no real understanding of the words that Jesus used. So we superimpose on His words our concepts, which come from our culture and our environment. We build our lives on our own conclusions and we create a belief system called religion.

Instead of reading *out of* the Bible, we read *into* the Bible. And we miss the Kingdom because of the noise in our heads.

HUMBLE AND TEACHABLE

Jesus had the perfect remedy for noise. He took put a child in front of his disciples and He said, "Truly I tell you, unless you change and become like little children, you will never enter the kingdom of heaven" (Matt. 18:3, NIV). Entering the Kingdom requires that you exchange your theology, your doctrine, your old religion, and your independent self-sufficiency for something new. Unless you change, you cannot enter.

Children are like blank pages. They know nothing. To become like a child means you need to stop being an adult.

Adults think they know a lot. Adults need to unlearn everything and start over. Unless you change, you will never enter the Kingdom.

> *Instead of reading out of the Bible, we read into the Bible. And we miss the Kingdom because of the noise in our heads.*

When a rich young man asked Jesus how he could be sure he would go to the Kingdom of Heaven, Jesus answered, "Obey the laws of the country of Heaven" (see Matthew 19:16-30). But the young man was rich in material possessions. He had obeyed the letter of the law, but he was not humble in his heart. So Jesus commented, "Truly I tell you, it is hard for someone who is rich to enter the kingdom of heaven" (Matt. 19:23, NIV). The young man was so used to making his own living that he was going to find it difficult to stop taking care of himself and let the King do it. He had been schooled in self-sufficiency, and it was tough for him to believe that God could supply his needs. His good life was getting in the way of Kingdom life.

In a way, we are like that rich young ruler. Our theology and our concepts occupy our minds and hearts. We say we want to enter the Kingdom, but we procrastinate. Not only do we need to listen to Jesus when He says we should become like children, we need to remember the first words of his public ministry, "Repent, for the kingdom of heaven is at hand" (Matt. 4:17).

The Kingdom has arrived. It is here already. If you do not change your thinking in time, you will miss it.

SEEK THE KINGDOM FIRST

If you seek the Kingdom of Heaven and its King, you will not have to worry about anything else—riches or poverty, sickness or health, life or death. In seeking the Kingdom, you are also seeking—and you will find—the pure provision of the King for every contingency of life.

Jesus said,

> *Therefore do not worry, saying, "What shall we eat?" or "What shall we drink?" or "What shall we wear?"...For your heavenly Father knows that you need all these things. But seek first the kingdom of God and His righteousness, and all these things shall be added to you."* (Matt. 6:31-33)

Another time, Jesus made it clear that anybody who seeks for righteousness will surely find it: "Blessed are those who hunger and thirst for righteousness, for they shall be filled" (Matt. 5:6). Once you find the Kingdom, you find righteousness, too. Your religious friends may not understand the change that has happened. Nevertheless, you will have found what you were looking for, and you will want to hang onto it.

In my experience, once people really know about the true Kingdom of God and they see it modeled, they want to get in. Citizenship in the Kingdom is a powerful lure. Most pastors do not understand the Kingdom so they do not preach it or teach about it. Consequently, most of the people in the churches have not entered into the Kingdom, and they cannot model it. Why should it be a surprise that nobody wants to join their church? What is surprising is that anybody does.

In seeking the Kingdom, you are also seeking—and you will find— the pure provision of the King for every contingency of life.

BECOMING A NATURALIZED CITIZEN

Seeking the Kingdom means seeking naturalized citizenship in the Kingdom of light. This is a completely new orientation for most of us. Once we attain citizenship, others will want to join us as immigrants, leaving behind the kingdom of darkness.

As in any other country, we can enter Kingdom citizenship through birth—"new birth." Many people call this being saved, but in terms of the Kingdom orientation, I think it is more helpful to think of it as birth. We call it being born again, and it is the same as changing your mind from rebellion to submission to the government of God. Through new birth, we become naturalized citizens of the Kingdom. New birth also naturalizes us in the sense that it seems to return us to our original, natural state of exercising authority and dominion over the earth.

When we seek to become citizens of God's Kingdom, we voluntarily align ourselves with a new government and a new country. We embrace its language, its ideals, and its values. A Kingdom lifestyle is typified by humility and prosperity at the same time, which is an appealing combination to the non-citizens around us.

And like any children, we are born into the line of inheritance that our Father has established. Everything in the Kingdom is inherited just by being born. Starting the moment you step into the Kingdom, it is as if you have a blank check in your hand at all times. You can't go off to a beautiful island and retire from the affairs of normal life, but inside your mind and emotions, you will feel that way, because your King will start taking care of your needs. That includes your need to have a fulfilling and meaningful life; He will give you assignments.

New birth also naturalizes us in the sense that it seems to return us to our original, natural state of exercising authority and dominion over the earth.

In the Kingdom, you will not have to protect anything anymore. When you accumulate your own stuff, you always need to worry about storing it. You may put in a security system. You've got to watch out. But the Kingdom brings freedom. Changing your mind and surrendering everything to the King brings you into a whole new place. That is why Jesus said:

> *Do not lay up for yourselves treasures on earth, where moth and rust destroy and where thieves break in and steal; but lay up for yourselves treasures in heaven, where neither moth nor rust destroys and where thieves do not break in and steal. For where your treasure is, there your heart will be also.* (Matt. 6:19-21)

Crime is impossible in Heaven, where there is no private ownership. No one can rob you anymore. Inflation and destruction can't get to the treasures you have laid up in

Heaven, either. Your life is free from stress. Whenever you lack something in your life, the King of Heaven furnishes it for you.

You may live on Earth in a colony of the Kingdom of Heaven, but you remain a full citizen of Heaven.

ADAMIC CITIZENSHIP RESTORED

We know that the first kingdom in existence was the Kingdom of Heaven. There was no kingdom before that one.

The very first citizen of the colony of the Kingdom of Heaven on Earth was the very first man, Adam. God took some dirt and formed Adam's body, and then He breathed the spirit into the body. Each one of us is like the first man, Adam; we have a body that comes from the earth and a spirit that comes from God.

God never intended that Adam, or any of us, would be considered citizens of the Earth, or even permanent residents. When I speak about Adamic citizenship, I am referring to a continuation of the original plan. What country is our citizenship in? Heaven. Do we expect to gain that citizenship status only upon arriving in Heaven after our death? Is it like retirement? Or can we experience heavenly citizenship right now? You know the answer: No matter where you go, your citizenship stays the same. You may live on Earth in a colony of the Kingdom of Heaven, but you remain a full citizen of Heaven.

But you also know what our problem is; we have become so used to the Earth that we think we are from Earth and nowhere else. And we become a little afraid of the very thing we are supposed to rule. Jesus was never intimidated by anything, whether it was a storm, or demons, or strong wind, or pestilence. He knew He was above all that.

It would not be disrespectful to say Jesus is like Superman. He came from another planet, so to speak, and when He got here, He had super powers. As a matter of fact, the Superman story is probably the closest story to explain who you are. You, too, are from another "planet," Heaven. When you came here, your powers kicked in because your only dominion is on Earth. When you go back to Heaven, you will not need your powers anymore. Kryptonite is sin. When you disobey God's laws, you lose your powers on Earth. Obedience protects you from kryptonite. It is that simple.

Adam was the first citizen from Heaven on Earth, and he was given all the rights, privileges, and authority of the heavenly kingdom, so that he could exercise dominion over the Earth. God gave him authority over the fish of the sea, the birds of the air, the cattle of the field, the creatures that creep over the ground—over all the earth.

We are supposed to be part of that same arrangement. We are from Heaven, and we live on the Earth, having brought all of Heaven's authority with us. For most of us to remember that we are really citizens of Heaven takes a major reorientation. Next time you walk into a meeting, engage in some kind of negotiations, or interview for a job, fix your mind on your true citizenship. "I'm not from here," you can say to yourself. "These people are being used by my government to fix me up. When I walk into this room, my King walks in too. Through me, He is in charge here."

WAKE UP

When you wake up to the fact that you were created to be a Kingdom citizen, lights will come on in your mind. You will leave behind the things that used to keep you stressed and discontented and you will look for opportunities to bring the Kingdom into the world around you. Paul put it this way:

> *Have nothing to do with the fruitless deeds of darkness, but rather expose them. It is shameful even to mention what the disobedient do in secret. But everything exposed by the light becomes visible—and everything that is illuminated becomes a light. This is why it is said:*
>
> *"Wake up, sleeper,*
>
> *rise from the dead,*
>
> *and Christ will shine on you."*
>
> *Be very careful, then, how you live—not as unwise but as wise, making the most of every opportunity, because the days are evil. Therefore do not be foolish, but understand what the Lord's will is. (Eph. 5:11-17, NIV)*

 *We are from Heaven, and we live on the Earth, having brought all of Heaven's authority with us.*

When you wake up and reorient yourself as a reborn citizen of the Kingdom of Light, the King will shine on you and His light will expose every last bit of darkness in you. He will expose your bad decisions, your irresponsible behavior. He will show you where you have been keeping bad company and how you waste money. Not only will He show you what is wrong in your life, He will go on to show you what to do about it. He will help you gather up all the knowledge and understanding you have accumulated, and He'll show you how to apply it.

Wisdom means applied knowledge. Knowledge and understanding by themselves are only comprehension, while wisdom is the application of that information.

The Kingdom is very practical. Everything you have learned up to now, the theories and principles, together with this great revelation you have gotten about the Kingdom, will apply to real-life situations. That is what Paul means above when he said, "making the most of every opportunity." Time is limited and evil has had the upper hand for too long. By continuing to seek the Kingdom with passion, you may find that the King will redeem everything you lost through your mistakes.

You will understand more clearly what the King wants you to do. He will organize your schedule and dictate the company you are supposed to keep. His will includes every detail of your life. The will of God should show you whom to be with and whom not to be with, and when, and for how long at a time.

At last you will understand why certain things had to happen. God will start to show you a vision for your life, your destiny in life. However, He will rarely let you see the steps of how to get there. This is because part of His plan is the process itself. He wants you to keep on exercising your citizenship privileges and to keep on trusting in Him. Joseph could never have viewed all of his seeming setbacks as steps to his destiny, but God knew what He was doing when He allowed him to be thrown in a pit—a pit that happened to be located just along the route of the slave traders who would pull him out and take him to Egypt. Go to the book of Genesis (chapters 37–50) to review the whole story. It is an excellent example of someone whose life belonged to God.

My point is this: all you have to do is wake up and stay awake in the Kingdom. The King will take care of the details.

By continuing to seek the Kingdom with passion, you may find that the King will redeem everything you lost through your mistakes.

MANAGING THE PLANET

The will of God for humankind is management all the way, just as it was originally with Adam. His will is not, as many of us believe, singing and clapping hands and going to churches. It is actually management. It's authority. It is taking responsibility for the things around us and bringing the Kingdom to bear on them.

As I have said already, every problem on the planet today is the result of mismanagement. Adam was given the original management contract for Earth and what did he do with it? He took the contract and gave it to an unemployed cherub named Lucifer, now better known as the devil. Adam took the authority and the territory that had been given to him and gave them to someone else. The devil "managed" the world into darkness, because he did not have any light from Heaven. Adam had to struggle for everything, and for all the rest of his life, he had one serious difficulty after another. Human beings have been following Adam's example ever since.

When Adam mismanaged his assignment, God took it away from him. The same thing happens to every one of us. Whatever we mismanage, we lose. Whatever we manage with God's help, we improve. Managing the planet does not mean that we become super-heroes or knights in shining armor who sweep away the opposition and conquer the world. Our management takes place in our own homes and neighborhoods, in our places of employment. We manage our own bodies by eating the right foods and getting enough sleep. We manage our marriages by spending time cultivating them. We manage our jobs and our salaries by getting to work on time and working diligently until quitting time. Thanks to the King's guidance, our steps take us to the right places at the right times. Once in a while, we know what it is like to be given a bigger assignment.

Adam lost the real estate he had been given to manage. We are being given a second chance. Now that Jesus has come as the Second Adam, our authority has been restored. The kingship of God has an opportunity to prevail.

When Adam mismanaged his assignment, God took it away from him. The same thing happens to every one of us. Whatever we mismanage, we lose.

We read in the constitution of the Kingdom that the earth is the Lord's. (See Exodus 9:29 and Psalm 24:1.) God never gave ownership of it to Adam, only the management of it. This was a good move, in light of what happened. God was wise not to give ownership to human beings. Sure enough, when the first man messed up in his management duties, God could work out another plan. He hadn't lost the planet altogether. If you manage somebody's apartments, the landlord still owns them. If you mismanage the property, the owner will simply fire you. He retains ownership and he can give management to whomever he wants to. He will look for somebody with a good track record.

I hope you realize that God does not hand you gifts from His storehouse just because you call yourself a Christian or even because you are righteous. He gives you what you need for your management assignment. He will let you keep managing what He owns as long as you manage it well. If you handle your money and other possessions well, He will give you more to manage. That is Kingdom thinking, and more we think that way, the better off we will be.

The Kingdom has come already. The Kingdom is here, now. It is present and functional on planet Earth.

THE KINGDOM IS *NOW*

Churches are filled with people who say the Kingdom is still coming. They believe that they will be in the Kingdom—someday. They think that the people who believe in Jesus will be full citizens after they get to Heaven, and that they must postpone their joy until then. "Thy Kingdom come" means we should pray for it to come, but it's not here yet, they say.

They are wrong. The Kingdom has come already. The Kingdom is here, now. It is present and functional on planet Earth and once you have been born again, then you have been naturalized as a Kingdom citizen. "Thy Kingdom come, Thy will be done on Earth as it is in Heaven" means that the Kingdom is alive and stirring already, and we are participants in it, bringing God's will to Earth.

Please wake up to the fact that the Kingdom is here and you have work to do. Do not lock the door against those who want to get in by telling them that it isn't time yet. Orient yourself to the idea of your full Kingdom citizenship. Pursue the Kingdom and its righteousness with a passion, and your life will overflow with Heaven.

CHAPTER 7

THE POWER OF CITIZENS' KNOWLEDGE

You can have a PhD in everything and still be stupid. It is not enough to learn information and understand it. You have to know how to *apply* what you have learned if you want to gain the highest level, which is wisdom.

In other words, the secret to a full life is not getting more knowledge of facts. People think they can get happiness if only they can learn enough truth. The Bible has this to say about such people, who are, "always learning and never able to come to the knowledge of the truth" (2 Tim.3:7). Knowledge by itself, even when the information is not false but true, is only the first step on the way to wisdom.

Knowledge is important, however, because it does need to come first. You need knowledge in order to get understanding and comprehension. Finally after you have grown in both knowledge and understanding, you are ready for wisdom.

Not only is wisdom the highest of the three, it leads us straight to the throne room of the Kingdom of God. Another verse in the Bible puts it this way: "Christ Jesus, who of God is made unto us wisdom" (1 Cor. 1:30, KJV). Notice it does not say that Jesus Christ is made unto us knowledge. Knowledge is only step number one. Jesus Christ is made unto us wisdom because His presence leads us into the full application of all truth and righteousness, in which our knowledge can come into play.

So we sell ourselves far short of all that the Kingdom offers.

KNOWLEDGE COMES FIRST

The fundamental importance of knowledge can be illustrated by a well-known story. Here is my version of it:

An elderly couple won first prize in a raffle: a free ten-day cruise. They had never been on a cruise before. In fact, they had never been anywhere, and they did not know anything about traveling. They had lived in the same dirty little house for decades and they had always pinched their pennies.

When they found out that they had won, they were so embarrassed. They did not know what to do. So they packed up a pitiful bundle of clothes, went down to the dock, and boarded the cruise ship. They showed their tickets, and the ticket-taker let them in. The man and his wife wandered around the decks of the ship, just taking everything in. They had never seen so much beauty. They had never seen people dressed so well. They had never seen so much activity. They had never used an elevator before.

They were shown to their cabin, which was on one of the highest decks, second from the top. When they got into their room, they touched their bed. They touched the floor. They ran their hands along the wall. They looked through the window and just stood there in amazement. It was like Heaven.

After they had settled in, they took out some crackers and cheese and packets of Kool-Aid. They mixed up a cool drink and just sat on the bed looking out the window as they ate. They were so excited to be on the ship.

Day after day it was the same. They would peep out their door at all of the well-dressed passengers running past, and they would close the door again and say "Yippee! This is wonderful." They would look out the window and see the ocean and say, "Oh, this is just like Heaven. And they would enjoy some of their crackers and cheese and drink some of their Kool-Aid for breakfast, lunch, and dinner, three times a day.

After five days passed, the captain became concerned. Two more days passed and he had never seen them in the dining room. Nobody had seen them at the clubs, at the shows, or anywhere on the decks. What had happened to those two people? He thought they had probably died in there.

On the ninth day, the captain became so uneasy about them that he sent one of his assistants to check on the couple. He knocked on the door. "Come in!" There they were, sitting on the floor on a sheet from the bed having a picnic on the floor. Wrappers from their crackers and cheese were all over the floor. They smiled up at him. "We are so thrilled to be on this ship. Thank you all, sir, for showing us your hospitality."

The assistant just stood in the doorway in shock. He did not know what to say when he realized that these people had never left their room for nine days. Finally, he gulped and said, "Excuse me, madam and sir, were you in this room all along?

"Yes, we are so happy. Thank you so much for allowing us to have this room. It's been wonderful."

He caught his breath and asked, "You never came down for breakfast, lunch, or dinner?"

"Oh, no, you see, we couldn't afford that. We are just glad to be on board."

He said, "You never came out of the room to enjoy the entertainment and extras?"

"Oh, no! We could not afford that, either."

Realizing something was wrong, the man asked to see their tickets. "Yes, sir," the woman said as she went to her purse, took out her ticket, and handed it to him.

He looked at the ticket, looked up, and said, "Didn't you read your ticket? Didn't you realize that your ticket gave you access to everything on the ship: all the food you can eat, all the clubs, all the games, all the swimming pools, all the Jacuzzis, all the spas, all the saunas? You could have had everything, for free...."

But by the time they finished talking, the ship came back to the dock. It was too late. They did not know in time.

How many people go their whole lives without understanding their country, Heaven?

When I first heard that story, it reminded me of God's cry for humanity in the book of Hosea: "My people are destroyed for lack of knowledge" (Hos. 4:6). I thought of the Kingdom of God, because it is the same with most of us, where the Kingdom is concerned. We do not know much of anything about it, even those of us who know we have got a free ticket. So we sell ourselves far short of all that the Kingdom offers. We skip right over the words of the Bible that explain the many ways the Kingdom works. We are as ignorant as new babies about the citizenship we have just been born into.

Now when you and I were real babies, we certainly did not know anything at all about our citizenship. I was born in Bain Town in the Bahamas, but I did not know a thing about the Bahamas for a long time. I was just a baby, blank. After a while, I began to learn things. As time went on, I began to understand what it meant to be a citizen of the Bahamas. It took a longer time to understand my citizenship in the Kingdom.

How many people go their whole lives without understanding their country, Heaven? Too many do not even know there is something to know about it. They could enjoy full citizenship, but they know nothing about how it works, what rights and privileges it brings, nothing about the laws. They stay ignorant all their lives and live on the equivalent of cheese and crackers.

My desire is for everybody to throw their cheese and crackers overboard and walk down to the buffet so you can enjoy the journey as much as the destination. The whole Kingdom is at your disposal; did you know?

LAW AND THE PROPHETS FULFILLED

All the knowledge contained in the pages of the Old Testament could not fulfill God's promises of restoration of the Kingdom—until Jesus came. As soon as He drew His first human breath, that knowledge—much of which was prophetic foreknowledge—began to grow into full wisdom. Jesus explained: "The Law and the Prophets were proclaimed until John. Since that time, the good news of the kingdom of God is being preached, and everyone is forcing their way into it" (Luke 16:16, NIV).

The Law and the Prophets were not superseded when the King arrived on the planet; they were fulfilled in Him. They represented the knowledge about the Kingdom, and Jesus brought the application of that knowledge.

If you skim the various books of the Old Testament, you will understand what I am saying here. Start with the "big five" books, which are known as the Pentateuch (meaning "five books"): Genesis, Exodus, Leviticus, Numbers, Deuteronomy. In these books, the ceremonial laws that God gave to Moses are laid out in great detail. Next we come to the book of Joshua, which describes the people of Israel after they had come into the Promised Land. Joshua's job was to settle the people and teach them the ways of God's Kingdom. As we proceed through the books of the Old Testament, the Kingdom story unfolds.

Every prophet, every judge, and every king in the Scriptures had something to do with preparing the way for the coming of the King. The judges and kings (the Law) embodied justice and the divinely human rights of the Kingdom. The prophets glimpsed the future and pronounced that a Messiah would come. Together, they represent the Law and the Prophets. Who were some of these people?

After the book of Joshua, the book of Judges gives us vignettes about the judges of Israel, men and women like Deborah, who took over an army and routed the invading enemy to protect the people who were being attacked. All of the judges of Israel exercised their power to ascertain and establish the rights of the citizens of Israel. The short book of Ruth appears next because it describes the lineage of the Messiah, naming His earthly ancestors. First and Second Kings introduce us to one of the greatest prophets of all time, Elijah, and his disciple Elisha. Both of them demonstrated the extreme power of the Kingdom of God more than the other prophets did. In fact, Elijah came to represent the very term "prophet" better than anybody else, just as Moses represented the term "law."

First and Second Samuel give us a look at the time when the people of Israel started asking for their first king. God wanted them to wait because He would be their King, but they would not wait. They wanted to have an earthly king like the other nations did. The prophet Samuel anointed Saul to be king, but Saul did not carry the crown with honor. Next came King David, who pleased God and ruled for a long time, giving us many illustrations of the Kingdom of God. The psalms that David wrote are all about Kingdom living. (Psalms are songs that show us how glorious God the King is. The book of Psalms is a book about a King, written by a king.) Besides establishing a kingdom that would become the model for understanding the Kingdom of Heaven, David himself was part of the lineage of the Messiah.

Even the two books of Chronicles, which record the history of political and military activities throughout the years, give us some insights into the Kingdom. When we read 1 and 2 Chronicles, we learn about good kings and bad kings, kings that worked out well and kings that did not, kings that pleased God and kings that failed to please Him, kings that built cities and kings that destroyed them. The kings became so corrupt that God began to send a series of prophets. Starting with the book of the prophet Ezra, we hear a common theme. It goes something like this: "Even though your kings and your countries are messed up, there is another King coming. He will set things right."

The whole Kingdom is at your disposal.

In the midst of all the kings and prophets, we have the book of Nehemiah, which is a book of restoration and hope. Nehemiah was neither a king nor a prophet, but he was a strong leader who fulfilled a vision to rebuild the city of God, Jerusalem. His accomplishments have never been equaled.

Not only do we see kings in the books of the Old Testament, we also see some queens. Queen Esther was one of the greatest leaders in history, male or female, and she exercised her authority well to preserve the seed of the Messiah. He was going to come through the nation of Israel, and Esther preserved the people, who were in the minority at the time, from utter annihilation.

The book of Job is an unusual one. In terms of the Kingdom, Job teaches us that no matter what God the King does, He is right. His Kingdom cannot be stopped by adverse conditions or by human stubbornness. Job shows us that the Kingdom of God is durable.

The book of Job is followed by King David's book of Psalms, after which we find the book of Proverbs, most of which was written by King Solomon, the son of King David. He wrote the book of Proverbs to show readers how Kingdom life is supposed to be. Tradition tells us that he also wrote the book of Ecclesiastes, which makes fun of the way people try to live without God. The summary of that book would read something like this: "Everything is a meaningless waste of time, except obedience to God. Live God's way and you will have long life." The third of Solomon's books is called the Song of Solomon, or the Song of Songs, and it is a long poem about the love between a man and a woman. Paradoxically, King Solomon did not follow his own advice even though it has been preserved for us in the Bible. He lost his kingdom because of his own sin. His loss does not contradict the knowledge and wisdom of the books he wrote for us. It only underlines for us the reality that the Kingdom of God is based on righteousness, because if you decide to ignore the King's instructions, you will lose what He has given you.

After Solomon, God stopped using kings to explain His Kingdom; from that time forward He used prophets exclusively to tell people about it. We have seventeen separate books, most of which were named after the prophets whose words are in the book: Isaiah, Jeremiah, Lamentations (also written by Jeremiah), Ezekiel, Daniel, Hosea, Joel, Amos, Obadiah, Jonah, Micah, Nahum, Habakkuk, Zephaniah, Haggai, Zechariah, and Malachi. These prophets demonstrated the power of the King even as they predicted the coming of the Messiah.

The book of the prophet Malachi is the last book of the Old Testament, and it ends with an announcement:

Remember the Law of Moses, My servant,

Which I commanded him in Horeb for all Israel,

With the statutes and judgments.

Behold, I will send you Elijah the prophet

*Before the coming of the great and dreadful day of
the Lord.*

And he will turn

The hearts of the fathers to the children,

And the hearts of the children to their fathers,

Lest I come and strike the earth with a curse. (Mal.
4:4-6)

God was closing out all of the centuries of prophecies by
saying, "There is someone coming before Me to introduce Me
to everybody." He was referring to John the Baptist, who would
announce the Messiah, Jesus, and who would come in the tradition of the great Elijah.

This is how all of the books of the Old Testament, from
Joshua to Malachi, deal with the announcement of the coming King. They saw ahead into the future and they announced
the Kingdom.

*Everything before John
was reference notes.*

After Jesus did come, live and work on earth for thirty-three
years, suffer crucifixion and rise from the grave, He was walk-
ing down a road with some of His old friends. At first they
did not recognize Him, because of course they thought He was
dead. As they walked, He went through the Scriptures with
them, explaining, probably in more depth than I did above, how
all of the early scriptures had to do with the coming Messiah.

When He finished, their eyes were opened and they realized He was the one talking with them. (The story can be found in Luke 24:13-34.)

THE LAW AND THE PROPHETS AND THE KINGDOM

Jesus had established these lines of connection well before that time. I have always been highly interested in something that happened on what we now call the Mount of Transfiguration. (The same story is told in three of the Gospels: Matthew 17, Mark 9, and Luke 9.) Jesus took three of his disciples up on a mountain. While they were with Him up there, who should appear out of the air but Moses and Elijah, who had been long dead.

Why those two? Because they represent the Law and the Prophets the most completely. Jesus did not take his disciples up on that mountain in order to show off His power. He went to have a meeting to pick up the baton. He went to close two books so He could open another. As He said in Luke 16:16, the Law and the Prophets were preached from the time of Moses to the time of Jesus' forerunner John the Baptist. Those are the only two things that could have been preached. But they pointed toward the Kingdom, which arrived on the scene with the Son of God, Jesus.

In other words, everything before John was reference notes. When Jesus came, the Law and the Prophets were fulfilled in him. Jesus was not destroying the Law and the Prophets. He was fulfilling them. The law-givers, law-keepers, and the prophets had fulfilled their duty. They had completed their assignments. The Law and the Prophets are vitally important, because they lead up to something greater, the Son of God Himself. Jesus said,

> Do not think that I came to destroy the Law or the Prophets. I did not come to destroy but to fulfill. For assuredly, I say to you, till heaven and earth pass away, one jot or one tittle will by no means pass from the law till all is fulfilled. Whoever therefore breaks one of the least of these commandments, and teaches men so, shall be called least in the kingdom of heaven; but whoever does and teaches them, he shall be called great in the kingdom of heaven. For I say to you, that unless your righteousness exceeds the righteousness of the scribes and Pharisees, you will by no means enter the kingdom of heaven. (Matt. 5:17-20)

Jesus came to bring divine wisdom where only knowledge and understanding had been before.

THE APPLICATION OF THE LAW AND THE PROPHETS

Jesus came to earth to set the people of the Earth back on course by bringing in His Kingdom, to fulfill all of the predictions and the foreshadowings that had come since the time of Adam. The prophets had spoken about a coming King. All of the earlier earthly judges and kings had portrayed Him to some extent. Suddenly He was here, and He won back men and women everywhere, inviting them to become His brethren, citizens of the Kingdom in the fullest sense.

Far from being as limited in scope and power as a new religion, His mission was to restore the Heaven to Earth. He came to render the application of the Law and the Prophets, to bring divine wisdom where only knowledge and understanding had been before. Here, listed for you, is a list of what Jesus' coming means for us. Jesus came to Earth:

- *To restore the government of God.* "For unto us...a Son is given; and the government will be upon His shoulder.... Of the increase of His government and peace there will be no end, upon the throne of David and over His kingdom, to order it and establish it with judgment and justice" (Isa. 9:6-7).

- *To bring back to Earth the laws of that government.* Every country is built on laws. The Kingdom is built on God's Law as given to Moses.

- *To bring the values of Heaven.* Every colony reflects the values and culture of its parent government, and the Kingdom of God is no exception.

- *To bring the citizenship of Heaven.* Once you get citizenship, you get all the others and once you get all the others, you have citizenship.

So when Jesus said to the people, "Repent, for the Kingdom of God has arrived" (see Matthew 4:17), He was saying, "Change your thinking, because another country has come back to Earth. It used to be here when Adam was alive, but Adam got rid of it. The prophets have been telling you that I would be coming, and now I have come. The reason I came is to bring that country back. That country is called the Kingdom of Heaven."

ADAM'S LOSS, JESUS'S GAIN

Because of what Adam did, human beings lost touch with the lifestyle of Heaven. Instead of living the high life, they started living the low life. Instead of living a life free from sickness, they became prone to sickness. Instead of living a life above depression, people lived under it. Humans lost the lifestyle that Adam and Eve had enjoyed in the Garden.

I am convinced that Adam never used to worry. Probably, he used to talk to the trees, walk on water, and speak to the fish. Why not? He had dominion over them. And when the Second Adam came, bringing back the original government of God, He too spoke to trees, walked on water, and spoke to fish.

When Adam sinned, God consigned him and his children and their children to toil and difficulties:

> *To Adam he said, "Because you listened to your wife*
> *and ate fruit from the tree about which I commanded*
> *you, 'You must not eat from it,'*
> *"Cursed is the ground because of you;*
> *through painful toil you will eat food from it*
> *all the days of your life.*
> *It will produce thorns and thistles for you,*
> *and you will eat the plants of the field.*
> *By the sweat of your brow*
> *you will eat your food*
> *until you return to the ground,*

since from it you were taken;

for dust you are

and to dust you will return." (Gen. 3:17-19, NIV)

Jesus turned this around. He modeled a stress-free (sweat-free) life. He showed us that in the Kingdom lifestyle there is no pressure to give you high blood pressure. When the men fished all night and caught nothing, He willed fish into their nets. (See Luke 5.) When He wanted to get rid of an unproductive tree, He did not have to sweat and use an ax to cut it down. He just said to it, "You will die," and the tree withered overnight (See Matthew 21:18-22.) When His men were in a boat that was sinking in a storm, He walked on water to save them. (See Matthew 14:22-33, Mark 6:45-52, and John 6:16-21.) He had complete dominion over the fish and the trees and the storms and everything else. And that is just part of what it means to have Kingdom dominion.

The Bible is like a contract or a covenant between the King and His citizens, and it tells us how to maintain our legal status.

KNOWING CONSTITUTIONAL RIGHTS

Before you can step into dominion you need to know the ways of this Kingdom. The first kind of knowledge you need is a knowledge of your constitutional rights in this new country. What rights have you been guaranteed under this government? How can you expect your life to be? How should you behave; what laws do you need to know about?

Because the Bible is like the constitution of the Kingdom of God, that is where we need to go to find out our constitutional rights. The Bible is like a contract or a covenant between the King and His citizens, and it tells us how to maintain our legal status. Of course we cannot follow its guidelines if we do not know what it says.

This can be a problem in any country. Have you ever read the constitution of your own country? The average person never does it. We have no idea what is rightfully ours, so we can't even argue for our rights from a legal standpoint. We do not even know when we have been deprived of something that belongs to us by law. (Have you noticed that most politicians are lawyers? They know something that the rest of us do not know, and they can use it to their advantage.)

A person who knows the law cannot be manipulated, and this applies to the Kingdom of God just as much as it does to other countries. The greatest example of this occurred when the devil tested Jesus in the wilderness. How did Jesus win? He quoted Scripture. (See Matthew 4:1-11, Mark 1:12-13, Luke 4:1-13.) He did not resort to rebuking the devil or binding him or casting him out. He just spoke a few words from the book of Deuteronomy and whipped the tempter.

*Dependency is the key
to our prosperity.*

The reason Jesus knew what to say is because He had immersed Himself in the written Word of God and the Spirit brought the right words to His mind when He needed them, just as the Spirit can do with us if we too read the Bible often and with understanding. Reading the Bible gives you legal power.

PROSPERITY GUARANTEED

Knowing what the Bible says will keep you from taking matters into your own hands. It will help you to trust the King to take care of you. Most of us have been raised in a society that teaches us to depend on nobody but ourselves. We learn how to protect ourselves and how to hang on to what we own. We find it hard to submit to anybody, and we do not want anybody else to run our lives. When we come into the Kingdom of God, we must change our minds and hearts or Jesus can't really help us very much. Yes, we pray and ask Him for help—and then we go and help ourselves. Our contingency plans are proof of the power of the spirit of independence. We pray and then we answer our own prayers. That is our old culture.

Yet dependency is the key to our prosperity. Remember how Jesus condemned the man in the parable who said "I have made myself rich! I must build more barns to hold my wealth." (See Luke 12:16-21.) Knowing what the Bible really says is the key to our dependency.

When I say that, I am not advocating the prosperity doctrine that some people preach. You can't just "name it and claim it" because you happen to want something nice. There is no such thing in the Bible as a prosperity doctrine. Jesus never preached on prosperity. He never had to, because in the Kingdom, it is irrelevant.

In the Kingdom, prosperity is a byproduct. When we seek first the Kingdom, all the things we need in order to prosper and flourish will be supplied for us. Getting into the

Kingdom comes first, and that places you in a position of complete dependence.

In independent-minded cultures, miracles do not happen as often, because people have their own contingency plans in their back pockets in case prayer does not work. When your trust level is low, your Kingdom life will be almost zero.

This bothers people, especially Americans, who see dependence on God as a copout. (That is the American term for it. Others would say it's a weak jelly-back way to live.) They do not appreciate the value of dependency. They do not understand that the lower you go before a king, the higher he lifts you. The lower you go, the more he exalts you. God is the King of the Universe. He owns it. The more you humble yourself before the Owner, the more you can expect to be exalted. Jesus said, "For those who exalt themselves will be humbled, and those who humble themselves will be exalted" (Matt. 23:12, NIV).

You know why more miracles happen in countries where the spirit of independence is not strong? Because in those countries, people do not have an alternative Excedrin to take. When you get a headache in a remote village in Africa, you need God. You can't get medical help. But in independent-minded cultures, miracles do not happen as often, because people have their own contingency plans in their back pockets in case prayer does not work. When your trust level is low, your Kingdom life will be almost zero.

STABILITY GUARANTEED

Those of us who live in the Caribbean know what happens when hurricanes come through. The only tree that does not fall is the palm tree. While the winds rip every other tree out of the ground by its roots, the palm tree will just bend down, even touch the ground, and come back up like an elastic band.

In the same way, citizens of the Kingdom, the people who have been planted in Kingdom soil will flourish in any kind of difficult circumstances. They are "the righteous," the ones who know the right way to live, the way of the Kingdom:

> *The righteous shall flourish like a palm tree,*
> *He shall grow like a cedar in Lebanon.*
> *Those who are planted in the house of the Lord*
> *Shall flourish in the courts of our God.* (Ps. 92:12-13)

When you place yourself under the government of the Kingdom and understand what that means, you will be living under a power than cannot be shaken by the strongest winds.

When economic problems come and wipe out everybody else, the Kingdom citizen will bounce back. Kingdom citizens are under a different system of government, a government that works *for* them. Kingdom citizens are like the Hebrews when God took them out of slavery in Egypt. (See Exodus 7–11.) God made the plagues attack all of the people who were not His chosen people. He can do that because He owns everything. He can tell a locust to eat only the crops of the Egyptians and not the crops of their slaves. To them as well as us, God says, "If you obey me, I will be your God":

> *If you listen carefully to the Lord your God and do what is right in his eyes, if you pay attention to his commands and keep all his decrees, I will not bring on you any of the diseases I brought on the Egyptians, for I am the Lord, who heals you.* (Exod. 15:26, NIV)

THE POWER OF KINGDOM KNOWLEDGE

One of the psalms says, "A thousand may fall at your side, and ten thousand at your right hand; but it shall not come near you" (Ps. 91:7). That means everybody around you can get laid off in a recession, but it does not have to touch you. You can go to bed at night without anxiety. The company you work for can decide to downsize, "rightsize," or go into bankruptcy and you can still sleep at night with confidence that your King is looking after you.

When you place yourself under the government of the Kingdom and understand what that means, you will be living under a power than cannot be shaken by the strongest winds. You will be protected and aided in everything you do.

I learned the powerful value of knowing my rights as a citizen when I first began my ministry in 1980 and within a few years, we wanted to start a radio broadcast. When we went to the station to inquire, they said, "Okay, no problem. If you can pay for it, you can have your program—during the "graveyard shift" between midnight and six in the morning. They told us that was the only time of day when they played religious programs.

I told them we wanted a program that would come on during drive-time in the late afternoon, about five o'clock. They said that was impossible in this country. It did not matter that we had the money to buy the hour and that we were legitimate citizens.

I did not give up. I went up the ladder. Even the top guys in the company said, "No, we can't do that." I went higher. I made an appointment with the government minister who was over broadcasting in the Bahamas.

A little constitutional knowledge can be dangerous!

I said, "Sir, this is what we want to do and the corporation says we cannot." I showed him our plan. He said no. He said it was impossible because it was not Bahamian custom to have religious broadcasting on during the daylight hours. So I had to get tough. I said, "Look, I am a citizen. I have a product. I have the money. I can buy the time, and it is my right to do so. As a matter of fact, I would not mind taking the government to court...." That got his attention. I continued, "If I take the government to court, I will win because the constitution says..." and I started quoting the constitution of the Bahamas.

Nobody had ever done that with him before. He promised to bring it up at the next meeting of parliament, and he did. After three weeks, they called me in. "We have never done this before, but we are going to let you do it." That is how we became the first group in the history of the Bahamas to play inspirational Christian music on the radio. Our program came on every Thursday afternoon between 5:00 and 6:00 P.M. It was called "Music to Believe In."

Then when we decided it was time for a television program, we had to go through the same fight again. Back to parliament, more fussing. Of course, in the end we were able to exercise our right to buy a daytime slot. Our program, which was called "Choices," came on every Saturday evening at 6:00 P.M.

In both cases, our fight was based on the simple rights that are guaranteed to every citizen in the constitution of the Bahamas. It shows how a little constitutional knowledge can be dangerous!

KINGDOM AUTHORITY

Jesus promised that when a person becomes a citizen of Heaven and therefore a member of His household, that he would give that person authority: "Behold, I give you the authority to trample on serpents and scorpions, and over all the power of the enemy, and nothing shall by any means hurt you" (Luke 10:19). That authority is not meant for overcoming only snakes and scorpions—it covers "all the powers of the enemy." Because of that authority, nothing will destroy a person who has it. What a deal!

That means that we can have authority to tread on every demonic power, every social resistance, every economic avalanche, every disease, every torment. We can become immune to anything that tries to harm us.

Kingdom authority refers to your personal rights to exercise your power through alignment with constitutional law. I consider it a very important Kingdom secret. You can't have this kind of authority unless you are a citizen, and unless you exercise it as a citizen. You can't fake it. The sons of a man named Sceva tried to do that once, and it did not turn out very well:

> *Then some of the itinerant Jewish exorcists took it upon themselves to call the name of the Lord Jesus over those who had evil spirits, saying, "We exorcise you by the Jesus whom Paul preaches." Also there were seven sons of Sceva, a Jewish chief priest, who did so.*
>
> *And the evil spirit answered and said, "Jesus I know, and Paul I know; but who are you?"*
>
> *Then the man in whom the evil spirit was leaped on them, overpowered them, and prevailed against them, so that they fled out of that house naked and wounded.* (Acts 19:13-16)

How many times do we step out in what we think of as God's authority only to find out that it was not? We get mixed up. We confuse power and authority, because we see power and influence all the time, but we see true authority in action less often. A drug kingpin is a powerful person who controls a sizable network of other people and assets. But in truth, all he has is a lot of influence. "The authorities"—the police and higher authorities—have legal authority over his activities, and they can win out over him.

The more you know about the Kingdom of Heaven and the more you step out on that knowledge, the better your life will be.

When the police move in on criminal activity, they wear or carry some symbol of their authority such as a uniform or a badge. Even to enforce simple traffic laws, the presence of their authority is indicated by such symbols. If you tried to stop traffic on Miami Highway, you could stand there in your street clothes and hold up your hand, but I do not think the 18-wheelers would stop for you. It sounds like a recipe for self-destruction to me. However, if you went out there dressed as a traffic officer it would be different for you. Your authority to stop traffic would be obvious.

Kingdoms have symbols of authority, such as the crown. The most important symbol of authority is the scepter. Queen Esther knew about that one. She may have been the queen of the land, but she had to follow protocol to the letter if she wanted to save the minority group her family was part of. Unless her husband, the king, extended his golden scepter to her when she entered his throne room, she would be killed for approaching so boldly without permission.

She risked it, and her people were saved. (The entire Old Testament book of Esther tells the story.) We can risk it, too, because we can come before our King as if we have put on the righteous garments of His Son Jesus, who comes with us. The death order gets cancelled, and we can make our request. The King's authority goes out with us to accomplish the thing we have requested.

It is all in Whom you know and what you know about His Kingdom. I can assure you—the more you know about the Kingdom of Heaven and the more you step out on that knowledge, the better your life will be.

CHAPTER 8

UNDERSTANDING IMMIGRATION AND MIGRATION

W hen I look around the Bahamas, I see a country that is being invaded by outsiders coming here any which way—legal or illegal—because the governmental system in their original country is not working. Of course, it isn't happening only in the Bahamas. Every week, people are moving and changing countries, seeking to improve their lives. If things work out for them in the new country, they stay and we call them immigrants.

These people are willing to leave behind their parents, their aunts and uncles, their cousins, and their friends; they make many sacrifices to uproot their children and adjust to a new culture and language. Emigrating gives them no guarantees of security or permanency, but they risk it anyway.

Although my country is attractive to many of these people, the system here in the Bahamas is failing a lot of families. They live on the edge of survival, anxious and disheartened about the future. I get phone calls.... "I've got three children and I lost my job and I have been looking for a job for six months. My kids are hungry. We are living off the Red Cross." On one island, families who can't afford to pay their electric bills are bringing their kids down to the local beach to sleep at night where the breeze is cooler. Without electricity, their little houses are too hot to sleep in.

Sometimes I think God is laughing at the governing authorities as they strive to make impossible situations better.

Even the best forms of government that people have devised are not working all that well. The very countries that are attracting the most immigrants have a lot of problems. For example, countries built on the ideology of free enterprise and capitalism have produced one of the highest extremes of rich and poor people, along with all the problems such as crime that come with that disparity in wealth.

I believe that our system of government is one of the best, but our safety nets have a lot of holes in them. Almost everybody is living on borrowed money, and they are chasing their tails trying to pay it back. Part of the reason is that democracy itself is built on distrust. That is why we have the "separation of powers" in the branches of government and that is why almost everything turns into a power struggle. Most new laws or improvements come with a downside.

DESIRE FOR A BETTER COUNTRY

Sometimes I think God is laughing at the governing authorities as they strive to make impossible situations better. In fact, I know He is. Look at this psalm:

Why do the nations rage,

And the people plot a vain thing?

The kings of the earth set themselves,

And the rulers take counsel together....

He who sits in the heavens shall laugh;

The Lord shall hold them in derision.

Then He shall speak to them in His wrath,

And distress them in His deep displeasure:

"Yet I have set My King

On My holy hill of Zion." (Ps. 2:1-2, 4-6)

Built into human nature is this desire for a better country. Yet no country we have ever had in the world can measure up to the King's country.

This search for a better country is in vain if you limit your search to the countries on the face of the Earth. In fact, the national situation from country to country is so volatile these days that the sooner you shift your allegiance to the only country that will never fail you, the better. We need to follow our desire for a better country straight to the Kingdom of Heaven. It is a good thing that there is such a thing as dual citizenship, because that is what you and I are going to have to settle for as long as we are living on this planet.

As long as your citizenship is on Earth alone, you can be only as secure as the country you belong to. Changing your immigration status and adopting Kingdom citizenship along with your earthly citizenship is the sole way to truly improve your lot. "My God shall supply all your need according to His riches in glory by Christ Jesus" (Phil. 4:19), wrote the apostle Paul. The King is the richest of the rich, and the people who step under His kingship can expect nothing but the best and the most consistent provision, starting immediately.

ALIENS

Immigrants are aliens. Not aliens from outer space, but rather people who came to the host country as strangers, often alone and often without many resources.

As long as your citizenship is on Earth alone, you can be only as secure as the country you belong to.

The Bible says that Abraham considered himself an alien. So did Moses. Along with him, so did Joshua and Caleb. Centuries later, Esther was an alien in the nation where she was queen. Deborah was an alien. Isaiah was an alien. What it comes down to is that we are all aliens. None of us came from here; we were sent here from someplace else.

In the letter to the Hebrews, we find a paragraph that looks back through history. It is about faith, but it is also about aliens. Look at what it says:

> *These all died in faith, not having received the promises, but having seen them afar off were assured of*

them, embraced them and confessed that they were strangers and pilgrims on the earth. For those who say such things declare plainly that they seek a homeland. And truly if they had called to mind that country from which they had come out, they would have had opportunity to return. But now they desire a better, that is, a heavenly country. Therefore God is not ashamed to be called their God, for He has prepared a city for them. (Heb. 11:13-16)

You and I are like them—citizens of a heavenly country, but aliens from the point of view of the Earth. We are people who happen to be located on Earth for the time being. At one time, we were "separate from Christ, excluded from citizenship" and "foreigners to the covenants of the promise, without hope and without God in the world. But now in Christ Jesus you who once were far away have been brought near by the blood of Christ" (Eph. 2:12-13, NIV).

Never mind what country you live in; none of them will be an improvement over your main country, which is Heaven. So although you may be a citizen in good standing where you live, you are also an alien there.

We need to recognize this fact before we have to find it out the hard way, migrating from place to place in search of the right one. You know as well as I do that sometimes migration does not solve a thing. One of the biggest failure stories in the Bible is the story of the Prodigal Son, told in the fifteenth chapter of Luke. It is a story about a willful migration, broken hearts, regret, and repentance. Like all of Jesus' parables, it is ultimately a story about the Kingdom. Here's how the story goes.

> *You and I are aliens from the point of view of the Earth. We are people who happen to be located on Earth for the time being.*

A widower had two sons who were young men. The younger son demanded his half of his father's estate and he took off for another country, expecting to find a better life there. Once he got there, he squandered his money foolishly and brought himself to ruin. Not only that, but the country he was living in started to have a famine. He was desperate, so this Jewish boy hired himself out to a local pig farmer, who made him carry pig slop all day long. He was hungry, and that made him even more desperate. Finally, he came to his senses and realized that he would have to eat his pride and return to his father, from whom he had fled.

This is a lot like the human condition, don't you think? Starting with Adam, we have willfully removed ourselves from our Father's house, even though the earthly country we find ourselves in is in famine, relatively speaking. The best the world can give us is pig food, and not enough of that. We can't trust the jobs we have or the supply of resources. No matter how wealthy the world looks on the surface, it is bankrupt.

The young man set his face toward home, rehearsing to himself what he would say when he met his father again. "I... will say to him, 'Father, I have sinned against heaven and before you, and I am no longer worthy to be called your son. Make me like one of your hired servants'" (Luke 15:18-19).

But he never got to finish his little speech, because his father was so glad to have him back. The father quickly ordered up the best robe and new sandals for his feet and put a ring on his finger. He told the servants to kill the calf they had been fattening for slaughter and to throw a big party to welcome home the son. The father restored his younger son to full sonship status in spite of all he had done.

If you know the story, you know that the older brother did not like this at all. In fact, he was angry about it. It is similar to what happens in our churches sometimes, when hardworking, loyal church members feel unrewarded for all of their efforts and refuse to celebrate when someone they perceive as a slacker gets too much attention. This older brother was legalistic and judgmental. He had always tried to do everything his father told him to, but he never expected any party—and in his jealousy he was determined not to participate at his undeserving brother's welcome-home party. He did not realize that he was every bit as foolish as his younger brother, but in a less obvious way. He did not know that God is not impressed by his lifelong hard work, even if it was in God's (or his father's) name.

Of course most of us do not want to identify ourselves with the older brother, but what it comes down to is that we are a lot like him after all. How does this apply to the Kingdom of God? Our Father, the King, is always welcoming his sons back, and we need to get used to it. Better still, we need to become better aware of our own status as a son in the Kingdom, so we do not have to run away to find out we left something good, and so we can live to the fullest as Kingdom citizens right here and now.

ONCE YOU WERE FAR AWAY

You and I are aliens either way. I know which kind of alien I want to be—how about you? I want to be an alien in my earthly country because of my Kingdom citizenship, and not the other way around. This is a very real choice and the Bible talks about it in so many words.

In our original state, we were not worriers. Kingdom people live by discernment and faith, not by their five human senses and their wits.

As soon as you and I receive our citizenship papers from Jesus Christ, we are restored back to heavenly citizenship status. From then on we will be aliens and foreigners in our earthly country, but we do not mind.

Our objective now becomes learning a new way to live. We have been restored not only in a legal sense to full citizenship, but also, like the son in the story, to full family status as well. It takes a while to unlearn a familiar culture and to learn a new one. In our case, we need to learn to live by faith instead of by sight. All our lives, we have been conditioned to live by sight. When problems come up, we look for solutions and we worry lest we fail to find them. We lose our jobs and we panic. We get a dire medical diagnosis and we despair. It can take years to learn a new way of thinking—which is the way of thinking that we were meant for all along.

In our original state, we were not worriers. Kingdom people live by discernment and faith, not by their five human senses and their wits. Nothing could be farther from the truth, because we have come back to our family. Not only have we obtained new constitutional rights, we have got the whole

Trinity—Father, Son, and Spirit—welcoming us with open arms, regardless of where we have come from, taking care of us.

Our pig-yard rags get exchanged for new garments, and—assuming we decide to stick around and abide by the rules this time—we can have everything we need, forever. We have obtained not only our legal citizenship rights but much more, because we are related to our Father.

Once you are back in the Kingdom, you no longer have to worry about anything. Every problem will be solved by your Father's government. All the wealth is common. It is a great country. Oh, and I should mention that the currency in your new country is love. Everything gets paid for by love. Faith works by love in Kingdom country (see Galatians 5:6).

ILLEGAL IMMIGRANTS IN THE CHURCH

Now to counterbalance that good news, I have some serious news for you: not everyone who seems to be a citizen of the Kingdom is one. It can be quite a shock to discover that the one place you thought Kingdom citizens would not feel like aliens, the church, is not much different from everywhere else. In fact, the church is full of illegal immigrants, people who do not even know that they are only pretending to be Kingdom citizens. They carry Bibles, dress up in nice clothes, and act nice. But they are illegal because they do not have Kingdom passports.

The biggest illegal immigrant that Jesus ever met was Nicodemus, the Pharisee. (See John 3:1-21.) If you will remember, Pharisees were religious specialists. They dressed right for the job; they prayed many times a day; they organized services. But when Nicodemus met Jesus, he had one question: "How do I enter your country?" He knew he was missing something.

Jesus told him about being born again, and we will talk more about that in the next chapter. But for now I just want to point out how many Nicodemuses we have in our churches. They perform their religious duties well, but they have no relationship with the Father. They can talk the talk, but they have not switched their citizenship to the Kingdom.

The King does not sit by idly while illegal immigrants erode the integrity of His realm.

They are a little bit like people who come to the Bahamas and try to act like Bahamians to fit in. They walk down Bay Street in front of the government buildings. They buy something from a shop. They eat some Bahamian food. They try to talk like a Bahamian ("yeah, mon..."), but none of that brings them even close to being a Bahamian citizen.

Some of these church people have been religious for a long time, but they have not changed kingdoms yet. Others may have been born again at some point, but they have not moved into thinking like citizens of their new country. They need to investigate what it means to become legal immigrants in the Kingdom of Heaven. It is never too late, but the sooner they do it, the better.

THIS KING WANTS YOU

The King does not sit by idly while illegal immigrants erode the integrity of His realm. In fact, the He does not hesitate to display the power of His Kingdom when necessary.

The apostle Paul, whose name used to be Saul, was an "illegal immigrant" at first, someone who was zealous in the extreme for his religion but who did not understand that he was fighting against the Kingdom of God. Having been a student of the rabbi Gamaliel, who was considered one of the top pharisaical scholars of the day, Saul was well-educated and motivated to make his fellow Jews follow every last one of the Hebrew laws. As a native of Tarsus, which was not a Jewish city, he seems to have been more determined than others to be the best Jew possible, and he was also a Roman citizen.

Saul could quote Greek and Roman poets. He had been exposed to a broader culture than many other Pharisees, but he was very narrow-minded when it came to the followers of "the Way," the name the early Jewish Christians were known by. In fact, he hated the Way with a passion. He felt it was distorting and perverting Judaism, and he was determined to defend his faith from what he considered a dangerous sect.

Using his influence in high circles, he obtained permission to hunt down followers of the Way. He wanted to destroy them before they became too influential. He knew he needed to hurry. The original band of eleven men had grown to a hundred and twenty people in the upper room that claimed to have had an encounter with this so-called Messiah Jesus after He rose from the dead. Then it had grown to five thousand and it as spreading faster than anybody expected. The "cult" was infiltrating the synagogues and people talked about miracles. Somebody had to stop them, and Saul wanted to be part of that effort.

He joined forces with others who were persecuting the Way, and they killed some of Jesus' followers. They drove other followers out of Jerusalem and nearby cities and scattered them across the Roman Empire. To hunt them down, Saul went to the high priest, "breathing out murderous threats against the Lord's disciples" (Acts 9:1 NIV), in order to get a letter of permission to travel to the great trade city of Damascus northeast of Jerusalem.

We are called to become Kingdom immigrants.

He and his companions made it into the city, but not as they had expected to. Before they arrived, this is what happened to Saul:

> *As he journeyed he came near Damascus, and suddenly a light shone around him from heaven. Then he fell to the ground, and heard a voice saying to him, "Saul, Saul, why are you persecuting Me?"*
>
> *And he said, "Who are You, Lord?"*
>
> *Then the Lord said, "I am Jesus, whom you are persecuting. It is hard for you to kick against the goads."*
>
> *So he, trembling and astonished, said, "Lord, what do You want me to do?"*
>
> *Then the Lord said to him, "Arise and go into the city, and you will be told what you must do."*
>
> *And the men who journeyed with him stood speechless, hearing a voice but seeing no one. Then Saul arose from the ground, and when his eyes were opened he saw no one. But they led him by the hand and brought him into Damascus. And he was three days without sight, and neither ate nor drank. (Acts 9:3-9)*

While he was there, God spoke to one of the disciples who lived in the city, an ordinary man named Ananias. He told him to go to a certain street and to ask for Saul of Tarsus, who would be expecting him. Ananias was fully aware of how dangerous Saul was, but he obeyed:

> *And Ananias went his way and entered the house; and laying his hands on him he said, "Brother Saul, the Lord Jesus, who appeared to you on the road as you came, has sent me that you may receive your sight and be filled with the Holy Spirit." Immediately there fell from his eyes something like scales, and he received his sight at once; and he arose and was baptized.* (Acts 9:17-18)

Saul's baptism signaled his switch to the Kingdom of God. His miraculous conversion changed him from being a legalistic, angry, defensive Pharisee into a tireless evangelist for the Way. He had an assignment to fulfill for the King. He was humble and contrite about his past. Soon he began to be known by a different name, Paul, which means "small" or "little."

He never looked back toward his former status as a leader of the Jews. He had become as much a full citizen of the Kingdom as those who had walked with the Lord Jesus in person before His crucifixion.

YOUR OWN IMMIGRATION

Although you and I will probably not experience such a dramatic conversion, we are no less called to an assignment in the Kingdom. We are called to become Kingdom immigrants.

It is my prayer that every reader of this book will be able to capture the spirit of the Kingdom and understand its culture and benefits more than ever before. May nothing stop you in your search for full citizenship. May you be eager to leave behind your old loyalties and seek adoption into the only country that can guarantee both your present and your future.

May nothing get in the way of its life-changing impact. May you attract others to it. (When people ask why you are different, you will have to confess that you are from a different country, because it shows in your actions and your lifestyle.) May your pressures and your struggles be consumed by the Kingdom and may the Lord give you a lifestyle that is so high and so unique that people will want to join you in citizenship in your new country. May they ask you how to get in—which is the topic of our next chapter.

CHAPTER 9

HOW TO BECOME A CITIZEN

God has been our Father from before our birth. Jesus is His firstborn Son, and the rest of us are meant to be Jesus' younger brothers and sisters. "He is the image of the invisible God, the firstborn over all creation" (Col. 1:15). You do not talk about a "firstborn," you know, unless other children are born after him.

Another name for Jesus is the Word: "In the beginning was the Word, and the Word was with God, and the Word was God. He was in the beginning with God" (John 1:1-2). This Word is the One who speaks words of life into each one He calls into His Kingdom.

I hope you know that you can't earn your way into His good graces. Kingdom citizenship is not like membership in the Kiwanis Club, where good works count as membership points. Many people make the mistake of thinking that citizenship in the Kingdom can be obtained through good works. They visit the sick and send money to Haiti. They attend church for fifty years straight. They take communion at six in the morning on Sundays and they sing in the choir. But none of that gets them into the Kingdom. It does not even crack the door open.

You can't become a citizen or a member of the family of God by good works or by association with His family members or even by longevity. You can try for ninety years and you will still be an illegal immigrant when you die. The only way to get into the Kingdom is to respond to an invitation. With the ears of your spirit you hear, "Come," and you respond to it by leaving behind your old ways of doing things and coming Home.

Kingdom citizenship is not like membership, where good works count as membership points.

It is just like physical birth; you leave behind the confines of your old existence and you enter into the endless possibilities of new life. The difference is that this birth is a birth of your spirit. In the words of Jesus: "That which is born of the flesh is flesh, and that which is born of the Spirit is spirit" (John 3:6).

The bottom line is this: you must be born into the Kingdom if you want to become a part of the family of the Firstborn.

FREE AT LAST FROM THE POWER OF DEATH

Rebirth means shaking free of death's grip once and for all. Remember that in the Garden there was no death—at first. But when Adam sinned, death came into the picture. That is why the Bible says, "the wages of sin is death" (Rom. 6:23). The world is filled with death. Death is the final punishment. We do not want to think about it.

But back in the Garden, the Father had already set in motion a plan to rescue the people He had created from their own sin. But to accomplish the plan, somebody would have to die. He asked His sinless, firstborn Son to do it. Then everyone who would accept the substitution could escape the punishment of death.

In other words, God decided to apply the penalty of sin and death to Himself. In God's courtroom, you and I were condemned to death. But the Judge said to His Son, "The judgment on these kids is death. I want you to go to jail for them and to be executed instead of them."

Jesus said, "I will go to jail for them. But is there any other way to do this?"

The Father said, "No, Son. It is either them or you." And the Son agreed to do it.

The Son, who was every bit as much God as His Father was, came to Earth as a man. He did it so that people like you and me would be free from the execution order. God's universal justice would be satisfied. It is as if you were sentenced to die in the electric chair and it is almost time for them to throw the switch when someone comes in and says, "You can get up and walk out of here. Go ahead. I will take the sentence for you." And he sits down in your place.

Have you ever thought about it that way? Have you ever realized that Jesus would have never died at all, even to this day two thousand years later, if He had not carried our sin to the cross when He died? Sin is what brings death, and Jesus did not have any sin at all, none. He was perfect. He was God.

*God decided to apply the penalty
of sin and death to Himself.*

But He went to the cross carrying our sins. Because of His overwhelming love, He shouldered the punishment for not only your individual sins, but for every sinful act that ever happened. The prophet Isaiah wrote that His body was so marred that it was hard to recognize Him as a man anymore. (See Isaiah 52:14.) Sin did that to Him. He was carrying all of our evil thoughts, our broken hearts, our diseases, our injuries, our wickedness. He did it to restore His Father's sons and daughters back to His family and to citizenship in His Kingdom.

The whole Old Testament leads up to the time when Jesus came to do that. People do not like to read parts of it, because it is all about blood sacrifices. Even back in the Garden, the first thing God did for Adam and Eve was to kill an animal so they could have clothing made out of its bloody hide (see Genesis 3:21). They had covered themselves with fig leaves. But leaves are not a good covering. Leaves do not have blood.

From that day forward, people began to offer living creatures to God as a sacrifice for their sins. All through the Old Testament they kept offering goats, sheep, heifers, doves, and more. Adam and Eve's sons, Cain and Abel, tried to work the sacrificial system. Cain brought an offering of vegetable produce from his fields, but Abel brought a lamb. (See Genesis 4:3-7.) The Bible says that God was displeased with Cain's offering, but He received Abel's offering. That does not make any sense to us unless we understand how God sees it. In His perfect system of justice, blood (death) compensates for sin, because sin is punishable by death. Cain's produce did not have any blood in it.

However, killing an innocent animal as a sacrifice is not the same as killing an innocent man. The penalty for sin was on humans, so God needed a sinless human sacrifice to serve as the ultimate payment for sin. Jesus was that sacrifice. And now, if we accept what Jesus did, these words can apply to our own lives:

> *We were therefore buried with him through baptism into death in order that, just as Christ was raised from the dead through the glory of the Father, we too may live a new life. For if we have been united with him in a death like his, we will certainly also be united with him in a resurrection like his. For we know that our old self was crucified with him so that the body ruled by sin might be done away with, that we should no longer be slaves to sin—because anyone who has died has been set free from sin. Now if we died with Christ, we believe that we will also live with him.* (Rom. 6:4-8 NIV)

In other words, once He died, nobody else had to die. His death paid for all that sin. In fact, it is as if He made it possible for us to be born anew. Now we can live forever, as if we never sinned even once.

This is the salvation story. If you want to make it your own story, you need to be reborn. Just as both water and blood are involved in natural childbirth, both water and blood were part of Christ's death (see John 19:34), and they signify every new life:

For whatever is born of God overcomes the world. And this is the victory that has overcome the world— our faith. Who is he who overcomes the world, but he who believes that Jesus is the Son of God?

This is He who came by water and blood—Jesus Christ; not only by water, but by water and blood. And it is the Spirit who bears witness, because the Spirit is truth. For there are three that bear witness in heaven: the Father, the Word, and the Holy Spirit; and these three are one. And there are three that bear witness on earth: the Spirit, the water, and the blood; and these three agree as one. (1 John 5:4-8)

BORN INTO CITIZENSHIP

You know you cannot be born for your children and you can't be reborn for them, either. Just because their parents are in the Kingdom of God does not automatically put them in.

You cannot become a legal citizen of the Kingdom because the King likes you. You must be born anew in your spirit by the power of the Holy Spirit.

A religious leader who talked with Jesus had been born into the religious community. He was in charge of the synagogue and I am sure he knew the books of the Torah by heart. But when he met Jesus, he knew he needed something more.

"Jesus," he said, "I would like to enter the Kingdom. What should I do?"

> *Jesus answered and said to him, "Most assuredly, I say to you, unless one is born again, he cannot see the kingdom of God."*
>
> *Nicodemus said to Him, "How can a man be born when he is old? Can he enter a second time into his mother's womb and be born?"*
>
> *Jesus answered, "Most assuredly, I say to you, unless one is born of water and the Spirit, he cannot enter the kingdom of God. That which is born of the flesh is flesh, and that which is born of the Spirit is spirit. Do not marvel that I said to you, 'You must be born again.' The wind blows where it wishes, and you hear the sound of it, but cannot tell where it comes from and where it goes. So is everyone who is born of the Spirit."*
>
> *Nicodemus answered and said to Him, "How can these things be?"*
>
> *Jesus answered and said to him, "Are you the teacher of Israel, and do not know these things?* (John 3:3-10)

Jesus told Nicodemus that the only way to get into the country of the Kingdom is the same way he got into the nation of Israel—through birth. No paperwork. No waiting. Of course this confused Nicodemus. It did not make sense to his theological mind.

So Jesus explained to him that his body was not *him.* His spirit was. His body was just a house for his spirit. His body had already been born. Now it was his spirit's turn. And just as a highly educated ruler of the Jews should already know that the best way to natural citizenship is through birth, so he should know that the way to enter a spiritual kingdom is through a spiritual birth.

A person cannot work for Kingdom citizenship. You do not have to pass a test or reside in a certain place for a specified length of time. You do not have to observe rituals, keep traditions, or follow rules. You cannot become a legal citizen of the Kingdom because the King likes you. You must be born anew in your spirit by the power of the Holy Spirit.

The word Jesus used is "see." He said that unless Nicodemus was born again, he would not be able to *see* the Kingdom. The Greek meaning is "experience." In other words, until he was born anew, he would not be able to experience the Kingdom personally. No one can understand a country unless he has been in the country, and no one can enter the Kingdom country to experience it unless he gets born again.

Now Jesus isn't saying that being born again is what we might call a "religious experience." It is a process, a pathway. In fact, this is the only time in the Bible that he mentioned being born again. Most of the time, He simply preaches that the Kingdom is here, now; the Kingdom has arrived. New birth is the avenue to citizenship in it.

Nicodemus was not making fun of the idea when he asked about entering a second time into his mother's womb. He was taking Jesus seriously. He was willing to try the impossible if only he could get into the Kingdom. He knew that no one would be able to tamper with his citizenship if it came through being born, because spiritual birth cannot be reversed any more than a physical birth can be reversed. As Jesus' disciple Peter wrote: "For you have been born again, not of perishable seed, but of imperishable, through the living and enduring word of God" (1 Pet. 1:23, NIV).

How would Nicodemus know he had been reborn? The same way you and I know—because we have the Spirit of Jesus inside our spirits. Jesus' disciple John answered that question this way:

> *This is how we know that we live in him and he in us: He has given us of his Spirit. And we have seen and testify that the Father has sent his Son to be the Savior of the world. If anyone acknowledges that Jesus is the Son of God, God lives in them and they in God.* (1 John 4:13-15, NIV).

When you become a citizen of the Kingdom of Heaven's colony on Earth, the King sends His Governor (the Spirit) to come live in you. Your body is like the governor's mansion.

Rebirth does not come with thunder and lightning and earthquakes. You may not feel anything or hear anything. No angels may appear to you. But that does not mean it did not happen. The Holy Spirit comes and no one sees Him. Then you walk into your house and suddenly all the sins you used to enjoy make you feel guilty. You have changed. The Kingdom of God has come in. Now you do not like the same things anymore.

Your citizenship in the Kingdom does not give you a physical sign, but it does change your disposition. A heavenly lifestyle comes with it. It starts right in the midst of wherever you live now. You do not have to wait for Heaven. (Heaven is not the King's primary intention for your life, or I think he would kill us off right away after we are born again so we can go straight to Heaven.)

Once, some Pharisees asked Jesus when the Kingdom of God would come, and He replied, "The kingdom of God does not come with observation; nor will they say, 'See here!' or 'See there!' For indeed, the kingdom of God is within you" (Luke 17:20-21). No one sees it happen when you are born as a citizen. When you are a citizen you do not advertise it with signs; you advertise it with life and culture. You do not have to tell people that you are a Christian, because they should be able to tell just by being around you. You have been reborn of the Spirit of God.

God does not leave it up to you to select from a buffet of beliefs and doctrines. His way of doing things is clear. Yes, we are narrow—and narrow is the way that leads to life!

OBEDIENCE TO THE LAW— THE KEY TO PRIVILEGES

After your rebirth, you learn how to be a citizen of this Kingdom by obeying the laws of the land. As we have already made clear, the Bible is like the constitution of the country, and the Spirit helps you understand what it says and apply it. The Holy Spirit will also help you understand how the Kingdom works.

With Him living inside you, you will be able to tell the difference between true citizens and those who are pretending to be citizens of the Kingdom. Plenty of people believe that Jesus was a good man and a famous prophet. But do they believe that He was the Son of the living God? Not *a* son, but *the* Son? Do they submit to His commands?

Obedience to His commands is impossible without the help of the Holy Spirit, you know. Just try this one, for example, without God's love inside you:

> *Love your enemies, bless those who curse you, do good to those who hate you, and pray for those who spitefully use you and persecute you, that you may be sons of your Father in heaven.* (Matt. 5:44-45).

> *Love your enemies, do good, and lend, hoping for nothing in return; and your reward will be great, and you will be sons of the Most High.* (Luke 6:35)

God does not leave it up to you to select from a buffet of beliefs and doctrines. His way of doing things is clear. Sometimes people criticize citizens of the Kingdom. They say we are too narrow-minded. Yes, we are narrow—and narrow is the way that leads to life! (See Matthew 7:13 and Luke 13:24.)

You have been adopted as a full member of the royal family now, and you do not need to live like an orphan anymore

What is that life like? Joy-filled, stress-free and a lot more. It includes a lot more than an insurance policy that will get you into Heaven after you finish your life on earth. "My God shall supply all your need according to His riches..." (Phil.

4:19). I want to wait until chapter 11 for a longer discussion of the rewards, privileges and benefits that come with being a law-abiding citizen of the Kingdom.

Citizens of the heavenly Kingdom obey the divine King, just as citizens of any earthly kingdom must obey their king. Those of us who live in democracies fail to comprehend this. We are used to criticizing our leaders as we get ready to vote them out of office. We are accustomed to negotiating and cooperating, because in a democracy you do not obey an authority as much as you cooperate with it.

You do not negotiate with someone who owns you and everything around you. You change. He does not.

TURNING AROUND

When you declare that Jesus Christ is the Son of God, your Lord and Savior, you turn your back on your previous "lords," whatever and whomever you used to follow. You have been adopted as a full member of the royal family now, and you do not need to live like an orphan anymore.

This turning is called repentance. Jesus considered it the only option when a person gets confronted with the Kingdom of God. Repeatedly, He said, "Repent, for the kingdom of heaven is at hand" (Matt. 4:17).

Now, even if you have been considered rich in the world's eyes, I hope you will be glad to trade your so-called riches for the priceless treasure of the royal house. One rich young man did not want to do it:

> *A man came up to Jesus and asked, "Teacher, what good thing must I do to get eternal life?"*

> *...Jesus replied.... If you want to enter life, keep the commandments."*
>
> *..."All these I have kept," the young man said. "What do I still lack?"*
>
> *Jesus answered, "If you want to be perfect, go, sell your possessions and give to the poor, and you will have treasure in heaven. Then come, follow me."*
>
> *When the young man heard this, he went away sad, because he had great wealth.*
>
> *Then Jesus said to his disciples, "Truly I tell you, it is hard for someone who is rich to enter the kingdom of heaven.* (Matt. 19:16-17, 20-23, NIV)

This man knew he needed something, even though he had everything the world could offer: money, a powerful position, youth and a healthy body, good morals and religion. The trouble was, he could not part with his wealth. If only he had been able to understand that he did not own any of it in the first place. If he had turned it over to the Kingdom government, he would only have been giving the government back its things.

It is impossible for a person to call Jesus Lord and own anything. If He is your Lord, He owns you and everything you possess. There is no private ownership. So you cannot come to Him and say, "I want to submit to Your government. I want You to be my King and Lord"—and still hold onto your money, your land, and your business. When God asked the rich young ruler to give it up, it was not because He needed it. You cannot give God something He owns already. He was testing the man to see if he thought he owned it. Apparently, he did.

The man did not understand wealth in Kingdom terms. Wealth in the Kingdom is not measured by accumulation; it is measured by access to what you need when you need it. Wealth in the Kingdom is for distribution. Kingdom citizens are conduits, not reservoirs. Instead of collecting and keeping everything, they give it away to others. As they give it away, more comes to them. Peter, after he listened to this conversation between the rich young ruler and Jesus, said,

> *Then Peter answered and said to Him, "See, we have left all and followed You. Therefore what shall we have?"*
>
> *So Jesus said to them…"Everyone who has left houses or brothers or sisters or father or mother or wife or children or lands, for My name's sake, shall receive a hundredfold, and inherit eternal life." (Matt 19:27-29)*

Wealth in the Kingdom is family wealth, and every member of the family inherits all of it. To make a play on words, you could say that Kingdom citizenship is inherent—because the citizen inherits everything in the Kingdom.

The rich young ruler hung onto his money and possessions because he thought he was wealthy. He was poor, compared to the barefoot Teacher he was talking to.

MEMBERSHIP TO CITIZENSHIP

When the rebellious, Prodigal Son came back to his father after spending his inheritance, his return marked his reinstatement into the family. (I told the rest of the story in chapter 8; it is one of Jesus' favorite parables.) He trudged into view of the family homestead, and he spotted his father running toward him. His father fell on his neck, kissing him, overjoyed at seeing him again after having assumed he was dead. The son had thought about what he would say:

And the son said to him, "Father, I have sinned against heaven and in your sight, and am no longer worthy to be called your son."

But the father said to his servants, "Bring out the best robe and put it on him, and put a ring on his hand and sandals on his feet. And bring the fatted calf here and kill it, and let us eat and be merry; for this my son was dead and is alive again; he was lost and is found." (Luke 15:21-24)

The son would have been content to work for his father as a servant. He was so ashamed and broken that he would have been glad to be allowed to be a member of his father's household, housed and fed with the working servants. A servant is not a member of the family.

But the father would not hear of it. His son had come home! The one who had rebelled and who had run away had returned. He welcomed him back into the bosom of the family and gave him certain items of clothing to prove it.

"Bring out the best robe," he said. And he covered his dirty, worn-out robe with the richest garment in the house. He put new sandals on his feet. And he brought out a ring.

We are all like the Prodigal Son. We were born to privilege, but we take matters into our own hands.

The ring is significant. When a king wants to give somebody government power, he gives the person a ring. The ring represents the power and authority of the government. This ring was the symbol of family authority, royal authority. By slipping it onto his finger, the father was declaring that he was now far better than a member of the household. He was restored to the full status of a son. As a citizen-son he could now use the family name again, and he now had full family rights, full access to everything the family owned.

CLAIMING CITIZENSHIP

As soon as the rebellious son turned toward home, repentant, it was as if he was reborn. He had been born to privilege, but he had repudiated it. He failed to appreciate it. As a result, he had to go the long, hard way around before he could return. You can be sure that this time, he stayed.

In many ways, we are all like the Prodigal Son. We squander the resources our generous Father gives us. We think we can do a better job of managing our lives if we turn away from Him. We were born to privilege, but we take matters into our own hands.

I always say a sinner is really a saint who does not know he is a saint. What if nobody had told us that we could return home to our heavenly Father? It would be as if Prince William had been separated from his parents and spirited away from England at birth, kidnapped. Let's say somebody brought him to the Bahamas, and he lived on one of our islands with a man and woman who claimed to be his parents. As a baby, he would not know any better.

He would grow up enjoying the things his village enjoyed, thinking it was wonderful. He would think it was a great life— fishing, eating coconuts, running up and down the beach. He would not know that he was royalty. He would not know the kind of wealth he could have at his disposal. Unless someone came to tell him.

None of us can work our way into the position that the Son so freely offers us. All we can do is surrender to the offer.

Let's say his real father, Prince Charles, finds out where he is living and sends his only remaining son, Prince Harry, to get him. You can see the connection here—your real Father in Heaven sent his only Son to fetch you back into His Kingdom, when you did not know at all that you were royalty and that you had a place waiting for you in the Kingdom.

Prince Harry suffers all the difficulties of the trip. He bumps along the rutted roads, endures the sand flies and mosquitoes, sleeps out in the open under palm trees. Finally he reaches the village where his brother lives and he locates the young man. Can you imagine him trying to explain who he is and why he has come? "Your father sent me for you."

"My father? That's my father over there under the coconut tree."

"No, that's your stepfather...."

Imagine trying to convince this young man that he is a multi-billionaire. It might take a long time. But if he could convince him to leave behind the village where he grew up, he could step into the inheritance that had been waiting for him all those years. He could claim his position in the royal family and spend the rest of his life doing what he was created to do.

None of us can work our way into the position that the Son so freely offers us. All we can do is surrender to the offer. "Yes, I will come with You. Just tell me what to do. Your Father is my Father. I say yes."

Have you said yes yet? It is never too late.

CHAPTER 10

THE RESPONSIBILITY OF GOVERNMENT

Antagonism toward the kingdom concept is very common, and I do not find that hard to understand. Just think of the tyrannical kings throughout human history. The quality of a kingdom depends on the character of the king, and if the king is corrupt, his kingdom will be corrupt as well.

Some parts of the Old Testament read like history textbooks, with lists of kings and their wars and what happened to them. Once in a while, a good king came along who reigned over a period of peace and harmony, but such rulers were rare. Most of the time, the people lived in the midst of upheaval and tumult, all because of their bad kings.

More than once, God spoke through His prophets to correct royal abuses, and in general He tended to include these instructions:

- A king must fear God.

- A king must not gather wealth to himself.

- Rather, a king must use his wealth to take care of the poor.

- In other words, a king must be benevolent toward his people, even loving.

Of course most kings have ignored the advice of the King of kings, carrying out their own schemes, making the same mistakes over and over. But their failure does not change the fact that love is the foundation of a sound throne. The requirements for a good kingdom hinge on the disposition of the king, on his character and integrity.

 *The quality of a kingdom depends on the character of the king.*

Unrighteous kings, on the other hand, oppress their people. This is why we have proverbs like this one: "When the righteous are in authority, the people rejoice; but when a wicked man rules, the people groan" (Prov. 29:2). The quality of a kingdom comes down to a question of authority and how it gets exercised.

AUTHORITY

A powerful leader forces people to do what he wants. Oppressive power controls people, restricts them, masters them by means of fear of punishment. The people groan. Authority, especially divine authority, is not the same as raw power. Authority is powerful, but it is not dictatorial. True authority is derived from God Himself.

I can think of seven qualities of true authority, and every one of them applies to a good king who exercises his governing responsibilities well:

1. *A person of authority fears God and submits to Him.* A leader's personal submission to God ensures that authority will not be exercised abusively. For example, a pastor who fears God and submits to Him will never take advantage of a woman or a child sexually, even though he is stronger and more powerful than they are. He fears One who is greater than he is, and he submits to His commandments.

2. A person of authority has high morals and personal discipline. Fear of God leads to a morally upright, ordered lifestyle.

3. *People emulate a person of authority.* People admire and want to imitate that kind of lifestyle. This makes leadership easier. A good example of this use of authority is parenthood. The model of the parents' good behavior becomes a standard for the child's behavior.

4. *A person of authority does not seek to benefit from someone else's success.* He or she will rejoice about someone's success, but the person in authority will not infringe on it for personal profit.

5. *A person of authority does not use other people to promote him/herself.* Similarly, the authority figure

will not try to ride on the coattails of someone else's success, using it to improve public perception of his or her effectiveness.

6. A person of authority does not expect anything from other people except their own success. People should not have to support a leader financially or in any other regard.

7. *A person of authority wants the people under him to become great.* He wants people to achieve more than he has. Jesus Himself said, "He who believes in Me, the works that I do he will do also; and greater works than these he will do, because I go to My Father" (John 14:12).

When Kingdom citizens are under attack, the King rises up to defend them.

When the person in authority is a king, all of his citizens benefit. The people in his kingdom do not need to waste time or effort defending themselves from his abuses and exploitations. The people are happy to serve his government. The entire nation rejoices and flourishes.

GOVERNMENTS PROTECT THEIR CITIZENS

It is a fact of citizenship that all reputable governments, whether they are kingdoms or some other form of government, protect their citizens from harm. Even when people are not within the borders of the country, their government takes responsibility for their welfare.

When two American missionaries were detained in an Asian country, the U.S. Navy moved ships into the nearest port. Military helicopters were mobilized. Diplomatic messages flew back and forth. It became a matter of international urgency, even a potential cause of war—simply because they were American citizens and they were in trouble in a foreign land. When one young Israeli soldier was captured by the Palestinians, the "incident" drew worldwide concern as it escalated tensions between the two governments. The government of Israel, concerned for his welfare, negotiated for five long years before they could arrange for his release, at great expense and increased risk.

If this is true of governments in general, how much more is it true in the all-powerful, love-motivated Kingdom of God? When Kingdom citizens are under attack, the King rises up to defend them. Why else, for instance, would He have spoken to Saul on the road to Damascus in the way He did: "Saul, Saul, why are you persecuting Me?" (Acts 9:4). Saul did not know he was persecuting the Lord. He was pursuing individual Christians, not thinking that their King would rise to their defense against him. The King was taking it personally.

A KING IS RESPONSIBLE FOR CITIZENS' WELFARE

A good king is personally responsible for the welfare of every citizen. This is not the case in a democracy. In a democracy, the leaders—the president or prime minister, the congressmen, the state or provincial governor, the city mayor or district councils—none of them lose any sleep if some of their citizens can't pay their light bill. When the electric company cuts off the power to those people's homes, the president still goes to sleep at night in his nice bed without worrying about those citizens. It is every man for himself, for better or for worse.

This cannot happen in a kingdom, because the king's reputation is tied to his people's welfare. He becomes personally embarrassed when any of his citizens are broke. He does not want them to have to ask for bread and water, because it makes him look negligent. It is as if they are telling the world that he has failed in his responsibilities, he has forgotten his promises, and he does not have the resources in the first place.

The King considers your welfare His responsibility.

Have you ever wondered about Jesus' famous teaching about not worrying about personal provision? Read this with the Kingdom in mind:

> *Therefore I say to you, do not worry about your life, what you will eat or what you will drink; nor about your body, what you will put on. Is not life more than food and the body more than clothing? Look at the birds of the air, for they neither sow nor reap nor gather into barns; yet your heavenly Father feeds them. Are you not of more value than they? Which of you by worrying can add one cubit to his stature?*

So why do you worry about clothing? Consider the lilies of the field, how they grow: they neither toil nor spin; and yet I say to you that even Solomon in all his glory was not arrayed like one of these. Now if God so clothes the grass of the field, which today is, and tomorrow is thrown into the oven, will He not much more clothe you, O you of little faith?

Therefore do not worry, saying, "What shall we eat?" or "What shall we drink?" or "What shall we wear?" For after all these things the Gentiles [those who are not Kingdom citizens] seek. For your heavenly Father knows that you need all these things. But seek first the kingdom of God and His righteousness, and all these things shall be added to you. (Matt. 6:25-33)

> *In the Kingdom, the King is bound by His own laws to take care of his citizens.*

You see, Jesus was almost incredulous that anybody in His Kingdom would worry about such things. He needs to remind people that He is more than able to provide everything they need. Their fretfulness sends a message that they do not believe He wants to do it. They should not be so worried, because they are citizens of the Kingdom.

He invites everyone to the most important benefits of their Kingdom citizenship:

"Come to Me, all you who labor and are heavy laden, and I will give you rest. Take My yoke upon you and

learn from Me, for I am gentle and lowly in heart, and you will find rest for your souls. For My yoke is easy and My burden is light." (Matt. 11:28-30)

The King considers your welfare His responsibility. In the Kingdom, the King has a personal interest in your mortgage payment. I do not know how He does it, but He takes a concern in every citizen, personally. He visits each one of us and lives with us, following through with every provision we need. He knows what each one of us is feeling. He can figure out our biggest needs. He is doing it right now, and He does it day and night.

In the Kingdom, the King is bound by His own laws to take care of his citizens. How many times in the Bible do we read something like this? "Here's what I will do, because I promised to take care of you." Even when He feels exasperated with His people, He feeds them and guides them as a shepherd guides his sheep.

Abraham knew about this when he tried to persuade God not to destroy Sodom and Gomorrah because his nephew Lot lived there. He knew that the Kingdom constitution (Scripture) said that God would never destroy the righteous with the wicked. So he kept coming back to God: "If you can find fifty righteous people in the city, you cannot destroy it...forty... thirty...." He whittled it down to ten, but even that small number of righteous people could not be found. At least he bought enough time to get Lot and his wife and daughters out of harm's way before the rest of the wicked city was destroyed by a firestorm. (See Genesis 18:22-33; 19:1-29.)

I wonder how many people in each of our families could be saved if we knew our constitutional rights. The Bible says, "The seed of the righteous will be delivered" (Prov. 11:21, KJV).

That means we can claim our children for the Kingdom, even if at present they are wandering far away like the Prodigal Son.

You have the full protection of Heaven regardless of what happens around you. You can always be sure that your government and your King are looking after your safety as well as your every provision.

PROTECTION ON FOREIGN SOIL

I made a point in chapter 3 of describing the power of a passport. A passport-carrying citizen has immunity from all sorts of problems when he or she is away from home.

With a passport, you have the authorization to "pass the port." A port refers not only to the place where ships dock, but also the airport, the customs booth along the highway, or, in the case of a Kingdom citizen, the "port" of Heaven. Your passport enables you to move from one jurisdiction to another with freedom.

Because the passport is actually the property of the government of the citizen, the entire power of that government lies at the passport-holder's disposal. Most of the time, people take their passports for granted. But when they have a problem on foreign soil, suddenly they do not.

For a Kingdom citizen, this means that you have the full protection of Heaven regardless of what happens around you.

You can always be sure that your government and your King are looking after your safety as well as your every provision.

Here is a simple example from my own recent experience: I was in Tulsa, Oklahoma for a meeting, and I was supposed to fly home to the Bahamas that same day. However, the airline cancelled my flight because of a snowstorm. This could have been upsetting, because I wanted to go home, but I knew God would redeem it somehow. I called my wife and my office and told them I had to spend at least another day in the States. I went down to the hotel lobby and a guy came up to me. He is a well-known singer and he recognized me from a time when I was in Tennessee, his home state.

"Hey, man, I have been looking for you for a long time!" he said. "I was supposed to be singing at a concert here and they cancelled the concert. Now I am stuck here. Can we have lunch?" We went to lunch together in the hotel. We conversed as we ate, and at the end of our meal, he gave me a $5,000 donation. I did not expect that! (Airline, you can keep cancelling on me, if this is what happens when I'm stranded!)

When you think you are alone, stuck in traffic with all the other drivers acting like they are crazy, you have got all of Heaven watching to make sure you are okay.

The Kingdom takes care of its own in the here and now, not just in the future, by and by. Yes, Kingdom citizenship carries with it a guarantee of Heaven, but in the meantime you get a personal security escort from the King and his angels.

You have citizenship, so you have a passport that lists all of the promises and provisions of your government. You do not have to go home to your country (Heaven) to be blessed. You do not even need to be in Heaven to experience freedom from pressure and problems. You can have it all right now.

Until I knew about the way the Kingdom works, I never could understand what Jesus meant when He said this: "Whoever causes one of these little ones who believe in Me to stumble, it would be better for him if a millstone were hung around his neck, and he were thrown into the sea" (Mark 9:42).

Now I understand that Jesus was making a threat. In essence, He was saying, "If you dare to touch one of my citizens, you had better commit suicide before I arrive to deal with you." Anyone who tries to hurt a Kingdom citizen triggers the King's anger.

Deep in the Kingdom constitution (2 Chron. 16:9), you can find this line: "For the eyes of the Lord run to and fro throughout the whole earth, to show Himself strong on behalf of those whose heart is loyal to Him." If your heart is right before Him, He is watching over you. When you think you are alone, stuck in traffic with all the other drivers acting like they are crazy, you have got all of Heaven watching to make sure you are okay.

You can also count on this one: "For He shall give His angels charge over you, to keep you in all your ways" (Ps. 91:11). Don't wonder why citizens of the Kingdom can go anywhere with confidence and peace; it is because they do not have to worry about taking care of themselves.

The government of the Kingdom takes care of its citizens when their earthly governments turn against them. Daniel's earthly government put him in a lion's den, but God's government put the lions to sleep (see Daniel 6). Paul's earthly government locked him up in a Philippian prison, but God's government sent an earthquake to set him free (see Acts 16). Your government may fire you from your job, but the Kingdom government will pay your bills while you are unemployed. The government of Heaven exercises divine power on behalf of its citizens.

We have built a belief system that is afraid of tough times. We want relief from the pressure. We forget that we too have been sent into the world; we are colonists of the Kingdom, sent to subdue and dominate the evil one, one victory at a time.

God interrupts evil activities all the time. You don't know about it, because nothing bad happens to you after all, and you do not even know something got interrupted. When Saul was breathing murderous threats against the Kingdom citizens in Damascus, he definitely got interrupted. I wonder if those citizens even knew they had been first targeted and then preserved. That is something to think about.

"FATHER, DO NOT TAKE THEM OUT OF THE WORLD..."

Now even a child knows that we are not living in Heaven yet. Regardless of how many times the King protects his own, citizens of the Kingdom do suffer persecution, mishaps, illnesses, financial hardship, hunger, and more.

During the first century, believers in Jesus got driven out of town and killed. They had family members taken away from them. They had their houses burned down because they believed in Jesus. As time went on, the Roman Empire clashed with the Kingdom again and again. Believers were brutally martyred. It is still happening in some places around the world.

No wonder the early Church prayed, "Come quickly, Lord Jesus!" (see Revelation 22:12, 20). If you were living under those conditions, you would want Christ to come right away, too.

Jesus prayed to His Father on behalf of believers, but He did not pray that they would escape every hardship. Instead, He prayed,

> *I do not pray that You should take them out of the world, but that You should keep them from the evil one. They are not of the world, just as I am not of the world. Sanctify them by Your truth. Your word is truth. As You sent Me into the world, I also have sent them into the world.* (John 17:15-18)

In our time, we have built a belief system that is afraid of tough times. We want relief from the pressure. We forget that we too have been sent into the world; we are colonists of the Kingdom, sent to subdue and dominate the evil one, one victory at a time. In the midst of the battles, it must be possible to be kept free in our spirits from the clutches of evil, even as we may suffer in our bodies, because Jesus prayed for us to be kept from the evil one. Therefore it is possible to live right to the end of life, preserved from the evil one's impact and influence. It is possible to brush aside fear of evil, because we know that our King is stronger than anything the evil one can throw at us.

Our King has obligated Himself to provide total defensive coverage to His citizens. He wins every time. He never leaves us to our own devices, although we often think we are on our own. Remember when Jesus was arrested in the Garden of Gethsemane. His disciples were with Him. Peter grabbed a sword because he thought, "God needs help!" and he cut off the ear of the high priest's servant (See Matthew 26, Mark 14, Luke 22, and John 18.) Jesus took time to heal it. Peter should not have done that. Shortly afterward, Jesus stood before Pilate and He explained, "My kingdom is not of this world. If it were, my servants would fight to prevent my arrest by the Jewish leaders. But now my kingdom is from another place" (John 18:36, NIV).

Jesus did not call His disciples or the angels to deliver Him, because the whole reason He had come to Earth was to suffer and die on that cross. Jesus was a king to the end, exercising his kingly dominion by *not* interfering with the plan of God, and giving generations of believers courage to face whatever they had to for the sake of the Kingdom.

He gives His citizens authorization to destroy the works of the evil one. In this way, the King enlarges His Kingdom.

CITIZENS' AUTHORITY

Following from all that we have discussed in this chapter, we can see that the government of God invests its citizens with divine authority. The King gives it to them. He takes a measure of His own absolute authority and He bestows it on the people who live under His authority.

Unless the King gives it, the transfer cannot occur. He considers it His responsibility to apportion His powerful authority to the ones to whom He has given assignments. This authority brings with it all of the strength, the strategies, and the wisdom necessary to fulfill the King's assignments.

Jesus' coming to Earth signaled a new level of the transfer of Kingdom authority. He started with His twelve disciples: "Jesus called his twelve disciples to him and gave them authority to drive out impure spirits and to heal every disease and sickness" (Matt. 10:1 NIV). Later He spoke of the authority He was giving to all believers: Here's how *The Message* version of Scripture puts it:

> *See what I've given you? Safe passage as you walk on snakes and scorpions, and protection from every assault of the Enemy. No one can put a hand on you. All the same, the great triumph is not in your authority over evil, but in God's authority over you and presence with you.* (Luke 10:19, The Message)

He gives His citizens authorization to destroy the works of the evil one. In this way, the King enlarges His Kingdom. He extends the purpose for which He came to Earth to His colonist-citizens: "For this purpose the Son of God was manifested, that He might destroy the works of the devil" (1 John 3:8). From the time we become citizens of the Kingdom, it is our job, too, and we need the appropriate divine authority to do it. He gives his citizens authority to go to the root of problems—the evil ruler of the world.

Jesus was going to be leaving the Earth for the time being. But, as He told His disciples, He was not going to leave us orphans (see John 14:18). He was sending His Spirit to dwell in them, and subsequently in us. Through His Spirit and in His authoritative name, we would be able to overcome the world (see John 16).

This heavenly authority is the foundation of all the benefits and privileges that come with citizenship in the Kingdom. The government of the Kingdom takes responsibility for granting it to each of its citizens, and the key to retaining it is righteousness on the part of the citizens. We have described how important it is to remain in right legal standing with the government if you expect to stay out of trouble; people who break the law lose certain privileges. But upright citizens do not have anything to worry about. Quite naturally, they can enjoy the benefits and privileges that come with their citizenship, without begging or bargaining for them.

In the next chapter, we will discover much more about how this works.

CHAPTER 11

THE RESPONSIBILITY OF CITIZENS

You are a citizen of a country on Earth, and I hope you are a citizen of the Kingdom of Heaven. Remember that your citizenship does not mean only that the government is responsible for taking care of you, but that you have a responsibility to the government as well. It is a two-way street, and the traffic goes both ways. Just as it is for you as a citizen of your earthly country, so also in the Kingdom of God are you held accountable to the government by means of its constitution, in this case, the Bible. You can be a much happier and more productive citizen when you understand your responsibilities.

Sad to say, many people do not want to shoulder their responsibilities. They are glad God has saved them, but they do not necessarily want to obey Him. They do not understand that their obedience is a way of expressing their appreciation. Jesus Christ Himself put it concisely: "If you love Me, keep My commandments" (John 14:15). They also fail to acknowledge that the rights that they enjoy as citizens, while they cannot be earned because they have been given as privileges, must be maintained through simple obedience to the laws of the land.

> *Remember that your citizenship does not mean only that the government is responsible for taking care of you, but that you have a responsibility to the government as well.*

SUBMISSION TO AUTHORITY

When you become a citizen of a country, the laws of that country automatically become your laws. As you submit to those laws, you submit to the authority of the government. By submitting to the laws, you are free to remain in the country for a long time, to move around the country for pleasure or business, and to enjoy the protections and privileges of citizenship.

Break even one of those laws, however, and your freedoms will be curtailed. If you have transgressed in a significant way, you may be incarcerated in prison. You may be deprived of your passport. You may be required to go through a long process before you can be reinstated as a free citizen. Jails are filled with irresponsible citizens who did not take responsibility for keeping the law.

Citizenship manifests the contract between the government and the people. The key to enjoying the privileges that come with citizenship is personal obedience to the laws of the country.

So these are the facts, if you are part of the country called the Kingdom of Heaven: (1) You are a citizen with legal rights to benefit from the constitution of God. (2) You have personal rights and authority to exercise your power as a citizen through alignment with constitutional law. The last phrase is the clincher. The secret to wielding authority in the Kingdom is aligning yourself with the laws of the country, in other words, obedience. You obey God for the sake of your life here and now (and not just in order to get to Heaven when you die). This is the Kingdom lifestyle, and maintaining it is your responsibility.

Authority is a good thing, and you never outgrow your need for it. Can you imagine a plant saying this to the soil? "That is enough. You have been holding me down for all these years. I'm out of here, and I am taking my root with me." What would happen if a plant did that? It would die, sooner or later. The absence of authority brings self-destruction.

Fish were created to submit to water. If a fish decides to move out from under its authority, you do not need to punish it, because it will die. The safest place for the fish to be is *submitted.* Surely you have seen a fish out of water. It gasps and flips and flops, trying as hard as it can to get back into water. I know people like that. They try this and that and wonder why nothing is working. When young people leave home too early, life can be very tough for a long time. It is the same principle. It is time to get back under authority.

Part of submission to authority is patience. When we fly, sometimes I listen to the pilot talking on the radio. That man needs to be completely submitted to authority. If the control tower tells him he cannot land yet, he goes into a holding pattern. His flight plan is very specific. He cannot deviate from it twelve inches in any direction without getting permission. He may not be able to see any other aircraft around him, but the people in the tower can see all of them, coming and going.

In the same way, the authorities over us keep us from crashing into each other—if we obey their directives. Freedom has boundaries, always. In the Kingdom, if the King says, "You are free to eat from any other tree, but do not eat from this tree," He has good reasons. Disobedience is not the best way to find out about the repercussions.

Fish were created to submit to water. If a fish decides to move out from under its authority, you do not need to punish it, because it will die.

AUTHORITY MAKES POWER LEGAL

We like to be around powerful people, but we need to ask ourselves, "Is this person's power under authority?" Power combines ability and energy and force, while authority is the right and permission to use that power. Authority is the right to use power effectively, not because you could, but because you should. Authority makes power legal.

Therefore, authority is more important than power. Teenagers may have the power to leave home, but they do not yet have the authority to leave. A person may be very aggressive and loud in speaking, but if they do not have authority, their words will not carry weight.

Submission to authority is what makes a person effective.

One time a military officer came to see Jesus on behalf of his servant who was lying at home, paralyzed and suffering. Jesus was willing to accompany him to his home in order to heal the servant, but much to his surprise the man declined his offer:

> The centurion answered and said, "Lord, I am not worthy that You should come under my roof. But only speak a word, and my servant will be healed. For I also am a man under authority, having soldiers under me. And I say to this one, 'Go,' and he goes; and to another, 'Come,' and he comes; and to my servant, 'Do this,' and he does it."
>
> When Jesus heard it, He marveled, and said to those who followed, "Assuredly, I say to you, I have not found such great faith, not even in Israel!...Then Jesus said to the centurion, "Go your way; and as you have believed, so let it be done for you." And his servant was healed that same hour. (Matt. 8:8-10,13)

Notice how the centurion addressed Jesus. He called Him "Lord," which indicates that he respected His authority. "Lord" is a legal term, not a religious term. It means "owner." In that culture, you would use that word for a king.

See also how the centurion's military experience gave him a more complete understanding of the way authority works. He was completely submitted to the Roman emperor and any other commanders who ranked above him. He had at least a hundred soldiers who reported directly to him (The title "centurion" is related to the word "century," which indicates one hundred.) Probably he had been watching Jesus as he worked in the village. He may have seen Him healing the sick, raising the dead, casting out demons, and more. Obviously, this man Jesus had power. Obviously some higher authority was guiding Him. He knew that a person's performance depended upon his obedience to the instructions he had been given.

So he made the leap from his natural observation to faith—and Jesus was impressed with that, declaring that the servant was already being healed, and commending the centurion to the people around them. A distance away, the paralyzed servant got up from his mat, healed and whole, without Jesus ever having had to make the trip to his house.

In the same way, if any of us want to experience God's best for our lives, we must get positioned properly—which is to say *under* authority—and our entreaties will be heard and answered.

When you submit to God's authority, He shows you what is next. He helps you change your behavior.

RIGHTEOUSNESS EXALTS A NATION

Jesus said, "Seek first the kingdom of God and His righteousness, and all these things shall be added to you" (Matt. 6:33). He wants us to seek first His Kingdom and, along with it, His righteousness. "Righteousness" is the same as submission to His authority within the Kingdom of God. By becoming righteous, you uphold the authority of the Kingdom—which in turn will uphold you. "Righteousness exalts a nation" (Prov. 14:34). This is nothing like other religions, where "submitting" involves trying to keep your god happy. You are not bringing gifts to an altar or lighting incense and chanting in front of a statue. You are not contributing money or going through all sorts of rituals to obligate your king to look after you. You are not appeasing the authorities.

When you submit to God's authority, He shows you what is next. He helps you change your behavior. He even helps you seek more of His righteousness. By remaining close to Him, you guarantee that the authority of the government of the Kingdom will be extended—through you—wherever you go.

When you keep the law, you secure your God-given authority over the kingdom of darkness. Evidently, hell keeps track when citizens of the Kingdom keep the laws of God. Demons will know who you are if you abide in the Kingdom righteously. You are in their computer. That means that you can cast them out with ease, because they know you by your Kingdom reputation.

The laws to which you are submitting are heavenly laws, such as, "Love your enemies, do good to those who hate you, bless those who curse you, and pray for those who spitefully use you" (Luke 6:27-28). So as you use Kingdom love, which is powerful enough to extinguish the powers of darkness around you, you keep yourself under the protection of God while fulfilling your assignment.

You know that hatred will shut down your faith, and so will blind rituals. (In Galatians 5:6, Paul says, "For in Christ Jesus neither circumcision nor uncircumcision avails anything, but faith working through love.") So you submit to the God of love even more completely, to your own benefit as much as the benefit of those around you.

You do not get things from God just because you ask. You get things from the government of Heaven because you keep the laws of the country. It is not enough to talk about the laws in church on Sunday or at Bible study on Wednesday—you need to read the law-book as often as possible and follow those laws faithfully. The minute you stop doing that, you start removing yourself from the King's protection and help.

A lot of people think they can get away with sins just because nobody's looking. That is audacious, to say the least. We come to God and say, "God, heal me (but I'm still going to take drugs)." Or we say, "I'm going to sleep with that woman I am not married to, but I want you to bless my business and pay my bills." We demand things while we are in disobedience.

You will be able to submit to someone's authority if you are able to trust and respect that person.

Instead of breaking laws and hoping you can get away with it, why not start obeying laws that you would not mind getting caught obeying? For example, see if you can get caught loving your brother. See if somebody can catch you paying your tithe. Let somebody catch you forgiving someone who hurt you, or spot you committing an act of kindness. Gossip about somebody who has lived with his wife for forty-two years without strife; that would be a wonderful thing to gossip about. The laws of this country are wonderful, every one of them. Do right intentionally all the time, and the King is going to bless you.

How to Submit to Authority

Submitting to the King of kings often entails submitting to those He has established in authority. You cannot submit to someone you are comparing yourself to or competing with, especially if you are interested in taking that person's position. By the same token, you cannot submit to someone if you are jealous of that person, or if you distrust that person. It just does not work.

A good king is willing to decrease so one of his subjects can increase. In other words, a good king is willing to move over and let one of his citizens exercise power. A citizen can expect this to happen. He should not feel the need to push and shove to get the king's attention, nor should he shoulder his way in with a sense of entitlement.

You will find it impossible to submit to someone if you think they are not as smart as you are, even when you tell yourself you are not influenced by such things. Naturally authority does not match up with intelligence, and still less with educational achievement. But pride gets in the way and you cannot put yourself lower than a person you want to correct all the time.

Conversely, you will be able to submit to someone's authority if you are able to trust and respect that person. You will indicate your submission by laying down your own agenda in favor of theirs. You will not feel the need to win an argument or negotiate an outcome. Instead, you will find joy in performing assigned tasks and asking for advice.

Sometimes people say to an authority figure, "The Lord sent me to work with you. I want you to be my mentor." That is not submission. Those people just want to gain a measure of respect and fame in the eyes of others, so they can take away some of your friends and followers. They have got their ulterior motives all worked out.

You will find it easy to submit to someone if you know in your spirit that God brought this person into your life. Your discernment will show you that the person will not take advantage of you, and that he or she wants God's best for your life. You will be able to tell that your own effectiveness will improve if you are under this person's authority.

KEYS OF THE KINGDOM

The laws of God are the keys to His Kingdom. Abiding by His righteous rulings unlocks the divine power that you need to live as a fully vested citizen of Heaven. Therefore, the more you can learn about his laws, the better.

This is a spiritual reality with very practical implications. It changes a person's lifestyle into a Kingdom lifestyle, and that lifestyle has authoritative power. Look at the connection:

I will give you the keys of the kingdom of heaven, and whatever you bind on earth will be bound in heaven, and whatever you loose on earth will be loosed in heaven. (Matt. 16:19)

You should not be living to make a living.

When you use the keys of the Kingdom to lock and unlock, bind and unbind, you are not responsible for the exercise of power or for the results. You are, however, responsible to obtain and use the keys in the first place. By submitting to the laws of the Kingdom, you surrender to the authority of God, and that sets you free from the burden of making things happen. Heaven will back you up when you turn one of the keys.

Citizens of the Kingdom have a responsibility to learn the words of the Bible. We need to read it often, because we tend to forget what it says. We need to read it more often than we read the newspaper. When the devil attacked Jesus in the wilderness, His responses came straight from Scripture. He said, "It is written...." (See Luke 4:1-13.) Those words were His keys to the Kingdom and victory.

Jesus said "Most assuredly, I say to you, the Son can do nothing of Himself, but what He sees the Father do; for whatever He does, the Son also does in like manner" (John 5:19). He exercised the keys of Kingdom authority better than anybody before or since. Yet He, true Prince that He is, wants nothing more than for the citizens of His Kingdom to exercise those same keys.

You need to do only two things: (1) seek the Kingdom in order to get into citizenship, and (2) seek the King's righteousness in order to stay in it. In other words, stay aligned with the King. When you stay aligned with the King and His government, you obligate Him to take care of you. All of the promises in the constitution remain accessible to you, as needed. Things that you would otherwise need to fight for will come your way with no sweat. That is why the Scripture reads, "Seek first the kingdom of God and His righteousness, and *all these things shall be added to you.*" Having all these things added means you will have a lot of unwanted things subtracted, things like bad health, stress, and anxiety.

You should not be living to make a living. Your priority should not be working and living just to earn enough money to pay your bills. Jesus has another perspective on such things. He says, "take no thought for them" (see Matthew 6:34). Instead of fretting about food and clothing and adding to an endless list of prayer requests, why not take His advice?

THE POWER OF OBEYING LAWS

Righteousness means obeying the laws of God, out of love for Him and with His help. The word "righteousness" means all of these things: right positioning under authority, alignment with authority, right standing with authority, fellowship with authority, relationship with authority, correct standing with the regulations of authority, and fulfillment of a king's requirements. In essence, obedience to the laws of any nation is a form of righteousness, and that obedience keeps you in good standing within the country.

With the keys of the Kingdom in your hands, you have access to the storehouse. As long as you keep those keys in your hands, you can go in and out as often as you want to.

You know what it feels like to transgress a law or a rule, how it makes your heart thump faster when you see the police or another authority figure coming, even if that person does not know what you did. You have a private judge on the inside that makes you feel guilty. You know that you are out of alignment with the authority because you violated a regulation.

The only solution is to re-engage with your authority, to get back under his legal protection. Seek to regain and maintain your alignment with the governing authorities, and you will regain access to everything in the constitution.

BENEFITS OF BEING A LAW-ABIDING KINGDOM CITIZEN

Citizenship is the key to empowerment, because it provides legitimate access to all the rights and privileges of a state. When you become a citizen of the Kingdom, your citizenship is registered in heaven (see Ephesians. 2:19). Therefore, you obtain all the rights and privileges of Heaven. With the keys of the Kingdom in your hands, you have access to the storehouse. As long as you keep those keys in your hands, you can go in and out as often as you want to.

This puts you in a particular category of citizen, and it is a powerful category. For you as a citizen of the Kingdom of Heaven, nothing is impossible. (Jesus said so; see Matthew 17:20.) You can move mountains.

Prayer itself does not get things done. Positioning in prayer gets things done.

BENEFITS OF PRAYER

Jesus told a story about widow who went before an ungodly judge (see Luke 18:1-8). He was the worst judge around, a man who did not fear God and did not respect people. In those days, widows were destitute. They had nobody to look after their rights or their welfare. They were very vulnerable. This particular widow was no different from the others, except that she knew her rights. She knew that she had a right to her claim before the judge, and she was unrelenting in her persistence.

When that little widow stood before that judge, she knew her stuff. The judge said, "No." She persisted anyway. The judge said, "Go away." She came back. She was not begging or weeping. She was making a request, because she knew what her rights were. She knew the judge was required to render them to her.

Most of think of the words "judge" and "judgment" in a negative sense. We think of judgmental statements and consignment to prison (or to hell). But when the Bible says Jesus was a righteous judge, it means He is the Judge who is always lined up correctly with the laws of God—the one who gives you your rights. Train your mind to think of Him as a judge who is a *rights-giver.* His job is to get you what is rightfully yours. The lawyer makes the appeal but the judge executes justice.

The better you know what is written in the law-book, the Bible, the better you will know what your rights are. I have been calling it the constitution of the Kingdom, because it tells you all of your rights, privileges, expectations, aspirations, and hopes—and it tells you what you need to do to obtain and attain them. If you know what the Bible says and you follow it, you will be a law-abiding citizen who will not lose your rights.

In our experience, the Holy Spirit is the Advocate, Counselor, or chief lawyer before the throne of God. We know that the Bible was written by the inspiration of the Spirit. This guarantees that the Spirit knows that legal document front-ward and backward. Because He abides inside of us after we become reborn citizens, we do not have to come before the Judge all alone.

It will not matter how loudly you beg for mercy and cry out for help, because God does not bless you because you cry; He blesses you because you qualify.

The Spirit brings the law to our remembrance, and He makes our appeal to Jesus, "[who] always lives to make intercession for them" (Heb. 7:25). He is praying for us, standing between Heaven's judgment and our sin. This is a setup for total success. How can you go into that courtroom and lose a case? Even more powerful, this intercessor is your brother. Before you even get to the room, He is praying for you. He is offering His own righteousness on your behalf. When you walk in, you do not need to say anything. The Holy Spirit looks at the Father and says, "According to what He did," nodding toward Jesus who took care of the matter on the cross, and the appeal gets finalized. Your Advocate does not bring up your name. He brings the name of the King who paid the price for you and who has been praying for you ever since. You have the whole government backing you up.

Prayer itself does not get things done. Positioning in prayer gets things done. The best preparation for prayer is your obedience to the laws of God. Many times, the reason God cannot help you is because you ask Him last. Only by staying aligned with the Lawgiver and Judge, through the work of the Spirit and Son, can you prevail.

Have you noticed that if you have just sinned, you are unable to find boldness in prayer? When you break God's law, it shuts down your prayer life. You have cancelled your right to appeal. "If I regard iniquity in my heart, the Lord will not hear me" (Ps. 66:18, KJV). The prophet Isaiah stated it clearly: "But your iniquities have separated you from your God; and your sins have hidden His face from you, so that He will not hear" (Isa. 59:2).

It will not matter how loudly you beg for mercy and cry out for help, because God does not bless you because you cry; He blesses you because you qualify. Believers have authority in prayer as long as they have maintained their side of their covenant with the King. The covenant is a legal agreement. You do not have to go before Him with theatrics or hysterics any more than a lawyer would go before a judge that way. You just have to be a citizen in good standing, and the Judge will hear your case.

Does that sound too legalistic to you? Did you think that Jesus' coming meant the end of the Law? I have news for you; His coming meant that the Law was fulfilled in Him. "Christ is the culmination of the law so that there may be righteousness for everyone who believes" (Rom. 10:4 NIV).

Everybody in the Kingdom is equal. The King does not listen to special interest groups, and nobody has to wear special Kingdom regalia to get his attention. Any citizen of the Kingdom has equal access to the King. He will act on the behalf of anyone as soon as He sees that Jesus is standing there on that person's behalf.

BENEFITS OF ACCESS

Let's say I am a multi-billionaire and you are my son or daughter. You ask me for your inheritance early. I am generous, so I give you a billion dollars, and I help you set up a bank account for it. It is a drop in the bucket for me anyway, since I have more than 30 billion in my own bank accounts.

When your sister says, "Daddy, I don't want my own bank account," I am glad because I would rather give her access to mine. It is the better choice. I will give her access to my accounts and she can write checks whenever she needs to. She will never run out of money, will she? This is the same as God's provision for His citizens. No wonder Jesus told His disciples not to take any luggage when they set out to preach and heal the sick: "Take nothing for the journey—no staff, no bag, no bread, no money, no extra shirt" (Luke 9:3, NIV). He will send His provision all along the way, because they have access to His account.

Righteousness—being in a right position with regard to the government of Heaven—is what guarantees your access. My first child cannot go to the bank and demand funds from my account. Neither can you go to the throne room of God and start claiming things that you are not qualified to claim. Citizenship and right standing give you rights and justice.

Righteousness—being in a right position with regard to the government of Heaven—is what guarantees your access.

Many people think that righteousness means staying clear of the big sins. (You know, don't rob a bank and don't murder anybody.) But righteousness covers obedience to every little law; it also means do not lie or deceive people, do not be jealous or envious, do not criticize or judge, do not murmur or complain. One murmur can shut the whole government down as far as your access is concerned.

Now one of the dumbest things a person can do is to get up in the King's face and start fussing at Him. That is called rebellion. The only remedy is repentance and humble submission. Do not forfeit your access to God. He loves you and He has given you the whole Kingdom:

> *The eyes of the Lord are on the righteous, and his ears are attentive to their cry.* (Ps. 34:15 NIV)

> *"Sit at My right hand, till I make Your enemies Your footstool."* (Ps. 110:1)

> *In all your ways submit to him, and he will make your paths straight.* (Prov. 3:6, NIV)

> *Now it shall come to pass, if you diligently obey the voice of the Lord your God, to observe carefully all His commandments which I command you today, that the Lord your God will set you high above all nations of the earth. And all these blessings shall come upon you and overtake you, because you obey the voice of the Lord your God....* (Deut. 28:1-2)

COME LIKE A CHILD

We complicate our lives so much. Jesus makes it simple. One time, he took a nearby child and used him to illustrate his point about how to enter the Kingdom and stay in the Kingdom:

> *Then Jesus called a little child to Him, set him in the midst of them, and said, "Assuredly, I say to you,*

unless you are converted and become as little children, you will by no means enter the kingdom of heaven. Therefore whoever humbles himself as this little child is the greatest in the kingdom of heaven. (Matt. 18:2-4)

Do you see? Our primary responsibility as citizens of the Kingdom is to remain childlike. Stay close to God. Do what He says. Trust Him. Stop worrying; your Daddy is taking care of you. Right now—morning, noon, and night.

> *You were not born to beg. You were born to collect. You were born to have access to endless supply because your Father owns everything.*

The enemy of Kingdom life is being an adult. Being an adult will kill you, because you take on the responsibilities of the universe and you are not equipped to do that. You are a child; get used to the idea. God is your Father and Jesus is your big brother. You thought that being a mature citizen meant taking on more responsibilities, but in the Kingdom, it means taking on less. Adults have to calculate, analyze, and explain everything before they act. Adults do not believe in something until they see it. Adults need a reason before they will believe anything.

Children, on the other hand, are quick to believe, innocent of strategic thinking, pliable. They put unquestioning trust in those over them. They are not at all impressed by status or money. When they meet a billionaire on the street they think he is just another old man like their grandfather. Children do not own much of anything, so it is not hard for them to give things up.

You never hear a child fretting about having enough money, because somebody will always take care of them. They take things for granted, and that is okay. When I was a child, we had eleven children in the house and my father was not wealthy. It never occurred to me or my brothers and sisters to worry about where our next meal was coming from. It just happened.

Kingdom citizens soon learn how to trust like a child. Our Father supplies our needs from the most amazing directions. Who, for example, would ever have thought that God's safety deposit box was the mouth of a fish? When the disciples had to come up with tax money, Jesus directed them: "Go to the lake and throw out your line. Take the first fish you catch; open its mouth and you will find a four-drachma coin. Take it and give it to them for my tax and yours" (Matt. 17:27, NIV).

You were not born to beg. You were born to collect. You were born to have access to endless supply because your Father owns everything. You are a family member, a member of His household. You are also a citizen. That gives you relationship status and also legal status. Your disposition with God gives you position with God.

When you come like a child to the threshold of the Kingdom, it is easy to get through the door. God created you to be a citizen of the Kingdom. Do your part and you will never regret it. Every citizen must make his or her own response to the requirements of citizenship. Nobody can obey the law for another person. I cannot stop at the red light for you; you have to do it yourself. I cannot pay your taxes. I cannot align myself with the laws of the Kingdom on your behalf, as much as I might want to.

Obedience to the laws of the Kingdom is both a proof and a demonstration of true love. The King is coming back someday, and He will decide who has been following His ways. He will not be impressed with the biggest churches or the longest list of academic degrees. He will look at the hearts of his citizens. "Did you love Me? Did you love others? Did you listen and obey My Word?" Those who can answer "yes" will dwell in the Kingdom for all of eternity:

> *When the Son of Man comes in His glory, and all the holy angels with Him, then He will sit on the throne of His glory. All the nations will be gathered before Him, and He will separate them one from another, as a shepherd divides his sheep from the goats. And He will set the sheep on His right hand, but the goats on the left. Then the King will say to those on His right hand, "Come, you blessed of My Father, inherit the kingdom prepared for you from the foundation of the world." (Matt. 25:31-34)*

Sheep or goats? I know which group I want to be part of, and I hope I will meet you there.

CHAPTER 12

CITIZENS AS AMBASSADORS

Everybody on Earth is looking for something. They do not know what they are looking for. They do not know how to describe it. They search everywhere. They drink liquor, smoke dope, go to parties and clubs. They change jobs, get a different spouse, or go back to school for more education. They read books and search the Internet for whatever it is that they are missing. What can satisfy this yearning?

Those of us who have found the Kingdom know what it is—it is the King. Once you find Him, you know you have found your long-sought desire, and from the first moment, you want to share the good news with others. He is alive! He loves us! We can know Him! The more we learn about Him, the better it gets. We want to communicate to all of the other searchers what He is like.

This King is both our God and our Father; therefore He draws us into His Kingdom and His family circle at the same time. Most of us remain right where we started out, within the same human families, living and working with the same people. But we are not the same anymore.

For one thing, we have become ambassadors. From searchers and seekers, we become, by some imperceptible means, representatives of our new King and His government, wherever we may reside. We may travel from place to place, or we may stay put for decades. Wherever we are, we bring a taste of Heaven.

BEING RELIGIOUS IS NOT ENOUGH

The goal of God was never religion, but rather something I call "rulership through relationship." I have described His original plan to have Adam and all the people who followed him rule over and manage the planet, and the close association between the words "dominate" and "kingdom," which you might call rulership. But rulership alone was never God's goal, because it must be based on a relationship with Him.

We come into the Kingdom of God exclusively through establishing a personal relationship with the King and His Son Jesus. The Son opened up the way to this relationship when He became a man Himself. His Spirit comes to live inside each one of us, and we begin a lifelong process of growing more and more into His likeness.

Not only that, we begin to carry the fragrance of Heaven wherever we go. The apostle named Paul summed it up best when he wrote:

> *Therefore, if anyone is in Christ, he is a new creation; old things have passed away; behold, all things have become new. Now all things are of God, who has reconciled us to Himself through Jesus Christ, and*

has given us the ministry of reconciliation, that is, that God was in Christ reconciling the world to Himself, not imputing their trespasses to them, and has committed to us the word of reconciliation.

*Now then, we are **ambassadors for Christ**, as though God were pleading through us: we implore you on Christ's behalf, be reconciled to God. For He made Him who knew no sin to be sin for us, that we might become the righteousness of God in Him.* (2 Cor. 5:17-21, emphasis mine)

Those of us who have found the Kingdom know what it is—it is the King. The more we learn about Him, the better it gets. We want to communicate to all of the other searchers what He is like.

We have not been saved from our old, earthbound lives simply so that we could become nice-looking additions to the heavenly choir. We have also been given a task to complete—spreading the Kingdom across the globe. We have been commissioned to show the world what the Kingdom of Heaven looks like. We have become diplomats for the department of Heaven that has colonized Earth. In short, we have become ambassadors for Christ Jesus.

You cannot represent someone you do not know. So that is why being religious is not enough. You need an ongoing relationship with the One in whose name you carry out your day-to-day duties. With His Spirit inside, that should not be difficult to carry out, but we seem to need reminders. Books such as this one are helping people remember, "Yes, I am an ambassador for Christ, and I know what that means." An ambassador must be connected to the one he represents.

Other people represent their religions (or lack of religion) too, but they do not have this kind of a relationship. That is why they resort to rituals and secret practices, to moral codes and dress regulations. That is also why, sooner or later, they admit that they are still searching for something more. They are not connected with the King, and He created them to be connected.

MORE THAN A MESSENGER

In diplomatic circles, although ambassadors often live in foreign countries, they keep in touch with their head of state back home. Almost without exception, they know that person well.

Ambassadors cannot legislate. They do not create new governmental policies or declare war. Yet they occupy a special position, government-to-government. Their words carry weight. They are senior representatives who have been invested with authority from their governing authority.

In the Scripture quoted above, the Greek word translated as ambassador is *presbeuo*, which means someone just like that. Paul uses the same word again in his letter to the church in the city of Ephesus:

> [Pray for me], that utterance may be given to me, that I may open my mouth boldly to make known the mystery of the gospel, for which I am an **ambassador** in chains; that in it I may speak boldly, as I ought to speak. (Eph. 6:19-20, emphasis mine)

Imagine that! Paul was locked up in prison without much hope of being released, and he still considered himself an ambassador for Christ. Although his freedom of movement had been curtailed, he was able to write letters such as the one he wrote to the Ephesians, he was able to speak with visitors and guards, and he was able to stay connected to the King through prayerful attention to the Spirit within him.

Ambassadors of the Kingdom carry the authority of the entire country. Their words have weight, and they know it.

VESTED WITH AUTHORITY

Elsewhere in the New Testament, another Greek word for ambassador appears. The word is *kerux* and it is commonly translated "preacher," "herald," or "proclaimer." Such a messenger has been vested with authority to convey the official messages of kings, magistrates, princes, military commanders to authorities in other places, and to perform duties on behalf of their sending ruler. Throughout the New Testament, God's *kerux* ambassadors are proclaiming the divine Word.

They were vested with authority by God the King to deliver messages and perform duties on His behalf, wherever they went. It did not stop after the New Testament times. You and I have been vested with the same authority. Jesus was speaking to us when He said, "I confer on you a kingdom, just as my Father conferred one on me" (Luke 22:29).

His meaning is clear—messengers and ambassadors of the Kingdom carry the authority of the entire country as they go from place to place. They do not carry only a set of diplomatic rituals or social niceties. Their words have weight, and they know it.

I never thought deeply about the word "confer" until it was used over me in a ceremony. Some years ago, I received the OBE (Officer of the Most Excellent Order of the British Empire) from a representative of the Queen of England. I had to bow and he put this thing over my neck. Then the governor pinned something on my suit coat, speaking as he did it, "By the authority of the Queen of England, I confer on you the British Empire." He conferred a whole nation on me. Now when I go to England and they see "OBE" on my passport, everybody jumps to attention. "Yes, sir, Dr. Munroe; is there anything we can do for you?" Those simple initials carry the weight of authority.

How you act and react will represent your citizenship. Remember that you have been appointed as the local ambassador of the Kingdom.

Every time someone becomes an official ambassador of a country, the same phrase is used: "I confer on you the Commonwealth of the Bahamas," using the name of the ambassador's country. Thus, that individual personifies the whole country.

We are official ambassadors of the Kingdom of God because Jesus has conferred the Kingdom on us.

AMBASSADORSHIP

You will never see an ambassador in a club or a disco. You will never hear that he got drunk and walked around in public inappropriately dressed or participated in some scandal. Such behavior does not befit the dignity of the office. Ambassadors choose their words carefully, and you will never see them explode in anger in public. Whatever an ambassador does, the global community will impute to the country he or she represents. The ambassador *is* the country.

This should be no less true for Kingdom ambassadors. We should be asking ourselves, "Am I representing Heaven?" as we walk around the food store, go to the gas station, or walk across the street. I think one reason we are not very disciplined in our lives is because we do not understand that we are carrying the weight of the country of Heaven.

Jesus said, "He who has seen Me has seen the Father" (John 14:9). In essence, he was saying, "If you have seen Me, you have seen my source." Can you say that? Why or why not? Do people have an idea of what Heaven is like when they meet you? You might be the only Kingdom believer in your workplace. Those people around you have only one source for their information about Heaven; you may be the only "heavenling" they know. How you act and react will represent your citizenship. Remember that you have been appointed as the local ambassador of the Kingdom in that workplace.

BENEFITS OF AMBASSADORSHIP

If you turn it around, you can see that when you represent another country, it is a good situation to be in. Yes, you must behave yourself with dignity as befits your office. But you will be permitted to enjoy all the benefits of your citizenship with additional benefits added.

For example, have you ever seen an ambassador driving an old jalopy with holes in his shirt? No, because the government pays all of his bills. If he needs something, he just asks. "No problem, sir. You are the ambassador."

The Kingdom lifestyle—clean living, love-filled, and truly joyful—is ours wherever we may be stationed on the globe.

Not too long ago, I went with a few others to Haiti. The Bahamian ambassador picked us up at the airport and we drove through the streets in an air-conditioned SUV. All around us was rubble. People were sleeping on the streets in the muck, just as you have seen in all the pictures. We just drove through all of that in air-conditioned comfort, sipping on cool drinks. The Bahamian flag was fluttering from the front of that beautiful SUV. I am sure that the people we passed were wondering what country that flag represented, thinking to themselves, *Wherever that flag comes from, I want to go there.*

We arrived at the ambassador's house in the hills. I said, "Wait a minute. Are we still in the same country that had the earthquake?" Yes. We walked into the house and someone served us a big breakfast of bacon, cheese, and grits, right there in the middle of all that poverty.

The ambassador took me to my bedroom and it was as big as a house. He said, "You can sleep here tonight." I asked if he meant me and the brother who was with me or me alone. "Oh, he has his own room. This is all for you." And he opened a curtain and showed both of us a big swimming pool full of blue water.

I said, "Don't you feel guilty sometimes, your Excellency?"

He said, "No. When you step into my car and drive through my gate, you enter the Bahamas." The property of an embassy is the same as the country it represents. It will always be as rich as the country the ambassador comes from. It will never have to be as poor as the country in which the embassy and the ambassador's house are situated.

As we sat eating at that breakfast table, the ambassador had said, "Do you want more?" and we said yes. So the cook came in with another big plate of food. We could have had even more if we had asked. There was no end of food—in Haiti, after an earthquake.

The ambassador never had to fly to the Bahamas for his bacon and eggs. He received it every day in Haiti. He did not need to go back to the Bahamas to enjoy a nice, air-conditioned house with a pool. He was experiencing the Bahamian lifestyle in a country away from the Bahamas.

Your assignment may seem insignificant to you, but the way you complete it is very important.

The Kingdom lifestyle—clean living, love-filled, and truly joyful—is ours wherever we may be stationed on the globe. The

King is taking such good care of His citizens that they are living like the Bahamian ambassador in a ruined world. He is at work inside us, making us look more and more like Him. His goal is to bring us to a place where we will have no corruption, no sickness, no pressure, no difficulties. He gives us a big taste of it now.

This is a culture of plenty, and it makes people want to come to God.

EVERY CITIZEN OF THE KINGDOM IS AN AMBASSADOR

As you go to work tomorrow morning or stop to buy something that you need, remember that you are a citizen of Heaven *and* an ambassador for the Kingdom of Heaven. This is important, because you will not be able to be much of an ambassador for the King if you forget your identity. He has conferred His authority on you, and He has given you an assignment, to represent Him wherever you go and to spread the truth about the Kingdom you represent. Can you do that?

I pray that you will be able to connect with the King on a daily basis, and that you will hear what He is saying to you. Your assignment may seem insignificant to you, but the way you complete it is very important. May your citizenship in the Kingdom equip you to be a true ambassador, and may the King commend you for your service when its time is over. "Well done, good and faithful servant! You have been faithful with a few things; I will put you in charge of many things. Come and share your master's happiness!" (Matt. 25:21, NIV)—those are the words I hope you will hear when you reach your home country, Heaven.

ABOUT MYLES MUNROE

D R. MYLES MUNROE was a beloved statesman and internationally renowned bestselling author, lecturer, life coach, and government consultant. His legacy continues to impact countless lives—individually launching people into lives of discovered purpose and unlocked potential, and corporately ushering the global church into a greater revelation of demonstrating the Kingdom of God. He, along with his wife, Ruth Ann, served as senior pastors of Bahamas Faith Ministries International Fellowship. They have two children, Charisa and Chairo.

Get — FREE E-BOOKS every week!

LOVE to READ club

JOIN the CLUB

As a member of the **Love to Read Club,** receive exclusive offers for FREE, 99¢ and $1.99 e-books* every week. Plus, get the **latest news** about upcoming releases from **top authors** like these...

DESTINYIMAGE.COM/FREEBOOKS

T.D. JAKES

BILL JOHNSON

CINDY TRIMM

JIM STOVALL

BENI JOHNSON

MYLES MUNROE

LOVE to READ club

DESTINY IMAGE